400 TOGAF® 9.2 Foundation Level 1 Practice Questions Volume 1

By Steve Else, Ph.D

Co-Author Michael Novak

© EA Principals 2018

Disclaimer

EA Principals, Inc., has developed these practice questions based on The Open Group conformance requirements for the TOGAF® Certification for People program. They are not official practice questions and have not been reviewed or approved by The Open Group. Official Practice questions are only available from The Open Group (see www.togaf.info).

The basic document used in compiling this book is *TOGAF® Version 9.2* Standard, referred to as "The Book" (ISBN: 978-9401802833), available at https://publications.opengroup.org/togaf-library/foundation/c182. The Book is also available in abbreviated/outline form online at www.opengroup.org/architecture/togaf9-doc/arch.

Boundaryless Information Flow™ is a trademark and ArchiMate®, Jericho Forum®, Making Standards Work®, Motif®, OSF/1®, The Open Group®, TOGAF®, UNIX®, and the ``X'' device are registered trademarks of The Open Group in the United States and other countries. All other brand, company, and product names are used for identification purposes only and may be trademarks that are the sole property of their respective owners.

Preface

Why is this book necessary? For one thing, no other such book exists. There is no source – anywhere, in any form or format – that provides a comprehensive set of exams to provide practice in taking the TOGAF® 9.2 Level 1 Foundation Certification Examination.

The reasons for TOGAF's rising popularity are many and varied. Good luck in soon joining the community of over 80,000 TOGAF Certified Enterprise Architects.

1. First and foremost, TOGAF has proven itself to be an effective industry standard framework and method for enterprise architecture. TOGAF succeeds in effectively aligning Business systems and processes, the data and information needed to facilitate business operations, the applications that manipulate the data/information for business use, and the technology on which the applications and data/information reside.
2. TOGAF is complementary to, not competing with, other architecture frameworks. TOGAF is not "either-or" – it can be "both-and."
3. Similarly, TOGAF can be used in conjunction with other, non-architecture standards and methodologies. Examples include the Baldrige Criteria for Performance Excellence, various ISO standards, the EA Kanban Board, the Government Performance and Results Act requirements and other strategic planning frameworks, and various dashboards and "balanced measures" approaches.
4. TOGAF provides a repository of best practices. As such TOGAF both promotes knowledge capture, sharing, and management within the enterprise, while at the same time demystifying Enterprise Architecture.
5. TOGAF is vendor-, tool-, and technology-neutral. As an example, TOGAF can be used in an organization's Application Architecture, irrespective of, say, the Customer Relationship Management application used by the organization.
6. TOGAF is not a "one size fits all" approach to enterprise architecture. TOGAF is tailorable and can therefore be used in a wide variety of types and sizes of organizations.
7. TOGAF is a framework and method for achieving the vision of "Boundaryless Information Flow."

Table of Contents

Overview 5
   The Open Group 5
   TOGAF® Training 5
   TOGAF® Certification Examinations 5
   Tips for Taking the Level 1 Examination 6
   Using This Book 7
   Other EA Principals Products and Services 7
   Questions 9
   Test 1 Answers 16

TOGAF 9.2 Level 1 Volume 1 Test 2 22
   Questions 22
   Test 2 Answers 29

TOGAF 9.2 Level 1 Volume 1 Test 3 35
   Questions 35
   Test 3 Answers 42

TOGAF 9.2 Level 1 Volume 1 Test 4 48
   Questions 48
   Test 4 Answers 55

TOGAF Level 1 Volume 1 Test 5 61
   Questions 61
   Test 5 Answers 68

TOGAF Level 1 Volume 1 Test 6 74
   Questions 74
   Test 6 Answers 81

TOGAF Level 1 Volume 1 Test 7 87
   Questions 87
   Test 7 Answers 94

TOGAF Level 1 Volume 1 Test 8 100
   Questions 100
   Test 8 Answers 107

TOGAF Level 1 Volume 1 Test 9 113
   Questions 113
   Test 9 Answers 119

TOGAF Level 1 Volume 1 Test 10 125

Questions 125
Test 10 Answers 132
About the Authors 138

Overview

The Open Group

According to its web page (http://www.theopengroup.org/aboutus), The Open Group is a global consortium that enables the achievement of business objectives through IT standards. The Open Group includes more than 400-member organizations, with a diverse membership that spans all sectors of the global economy — customers, systems and solutions suppliers, tool vendors, integrators and consultants, as well as academics and researchers.

The Open Group Mission Statement states that the mission of The Open Group is to drive the creation of Boundaryless Information Flow™ by: working with customers to capture, understand, and address current and emerging requirements, establishing policies, and sharing best practices; working with suppliers, consortia, and standards bodies to develop consensus and facilitate interoperability, to evolve and integrate specifications and open source technologies; offering a comprehensive set of services to enhance the operational efficiency of consortia; and developing and operating the industry's premier certification service and encouraging procurement of certified products.

TOGAF® Training

This book is meant to be a supplement to – and in no way a substitute for – formal TOGAF® training courses, rigorous self-study, and hands-on application and implementation of TOGAF®. Mastery of the practice questions included herein is no guarantee that the reader will pass the TOGAF® 9 Level 1 certification examination. There is no substitute for formal TOGAF® training, conducted by a training organization that has been accredited by The Open Group, and actual experience applying TOGAF®. Formal TOGAF® training is conducted by a number of organizations, including EA Principals, Inc. That training is meant to prepare students to pass the TOGAF® Level 1 (Foundation) or Level 2 (Certified) certification exam, or both.

TOGAF® Certification Examinations

The Level 1 and Level 2 examinations are very different. While both examinations are multiple-choice, the approaches taken by the respective exams are different. For example, Level 1 questions are pretty much objective, and deal with basic concepts and components of TOGAF®; questions in the Level 1 examination require understanding of the Components of TOGAF®, in particular the Architecture Development Method. Level 2 questions require in-depth understanding of how to apply TOGAF®; the questions ask how you would apply TOGAF® in a scenario to improve a situation or to resolve an issue.

The Level 1 examination is closed-book; you may not use any reference materials or notes. The Level 2 examination is open-book; a PDF version of the TOGAF® 9 Standard will be provided for your use during the examination. That said, because of the length of the TOGAF® Standard, and because of the time limit imposed for taking the examination, few test-takers have the time to use the Standard during the examination.

In the Level 1 examination, there are 40 multiple-choice questions. Your response to each question is either correct or incorrect. You will need a minimum of 22 correct responses (55%) to pass the Level 1 examination.

Tips for Taking the Level 1 Examination

There are a number of factors that will help you pass the Level 1 examination. One proven approach for taking the Level 1 examination begins with achieving a thorough understanding of the fundamental concepts of TOGAF. First and foremost, there is no substitute for good training. Be sure to take a TOGAF training course from a training organization that has been accredited by The Open Group. The "accredited" part is very important: Accreditation tells you that a training organization has undergone a rigorous evaluation by The Open Group and has been found to be in full compliance with all The Open Group's quality and accreditation requirements.

Experience: If you are in a position to acquire hands-on experience implementing, applying, or managing a TOGAF system, this will be of great benefit. If you are not in such a position, a brief assignment to your Enterprise Architecture department could be one way to acquire experience.

Becoming "test savvy": Knowing the structure of the examination and how to attack the questions is often the key to success in taking a test. The first of these topics is addressed in the preceding section; the second, how to attack the questions, is addressed below. It is important to know that, unlike some examinations, the TOGAF certification examinations do not impose a penalty for incorrect responses. Accordingly, answer all questions – even if you have to guess.

Practice: The practice questions in this book are similar to the types of questions you will see on the TOGAF Level 1 examination. Use these practice questions to know more about the examination, and to increase your understanding of TOGAF. Please don't simply memorize the correct answers and expect to see the same questions on the examination. Understanding why the correct answers are correct is the key to successful use of this book. Using practice questions also helps with the next factor – time management. Answer the questions in groups of 40; time yourself to make sure you can finish in the required 60 minutes.

Time Management: The TOGAF Level 1 examination is timed – you will be allowed 60 minutes to complete the examination. You will not be allowed to take your wristwatch (or anything else) into the examination with you. But there will be a "Time Remaining" clock on your computer screen when you take the exam. Pay attention to it!

Should you answer each question before moving to the next one? If that is how you take tests, then by all means use that approach. But remember: the more time you spend on one question, the less you will have to spend on the others. Also remember that you may skip questions and go back and answer them later. You may also go back and change your answers at any time before you either press the "Complete" button or you run out of time. Most candidates who take the TOGAF examinations go through the examination several times. First, they answer the questions that they are sure about. Then they answer the ones they are not quite sure about, and then the ones they really are not sure about. Then they guess on the ones about which they have no clue. When dealing with the questions they are not quite sure about or really not sure about, they first try to identify and eliminate any "distractor" questions – those that have absolutely nothing to do with the question. Then they put the other three answers in order of how likely they are as the correct answer. Then they pick the one that appears most correct.

Taking both Level 1 and Level 2 examinations in "Combined" mode: While both Level 1 and Level 2 examinations can be taken in a Combined examination, we do not recommend this. The most important reason is that a huge mental paradigm shift is required when going from the Level 1 examination format to the Level 2 format. In particular, the Level 1 examination requires more linear, "left-brain" thinking, while the

Level 2 examination requires more complex, "right-brain" approaches to issues and problems. We recommend that candidates study for the Level 1 examination, pass the examination, and then spend some time studying for the Level 2 examination to get into the right "mind-set" for that examination.

Using This Book

This book is conveniently divided into a number of sections that correspond to sections of the TOGAF 9.2 Standard. Each of these sections is represented proportionally in the Level 1 exam based on its relative importance as follows:

- Basic Concepts (3 questions)
- Core Concepts (3 questions)
- Introduction to the ADM (3 questions)
- The Enterprise Continuum and Tools (4 questions)
- The ADM Phases (9 questions)
- ADM Guidelines and Techniques (6 questions)
- Architecture Governance (4 questions)
- Architecture Views, Viewpoints, and Stakeholders (2 questions)
- Building Blocks (2 questions)
- ADM Deliverables (2 questions)
- TOGAF Reference Models (2 questions)

The distribution of questions should provide guidance as to where to focus your study. Specifically, fully 20 (50%) of the examination questions are directly related to the TOGAF Architecture Development Method (ADM) – 24 (60%), if you count the Architecture Governance questions.

Other EA Principals Products and Services

In addition to this book, EA Principals, Inc., offers a companion volume of 40 practice scenarios to help candidates prepare to take the TOGAF® Level 2 (Certification) examination.

EA Principals also provides TOGAF® training courses to provide the knowledge required to pass the Level 1 and Level 2 examinations. These courses can be taken as private courses (i.e., presented at your organization – and specifically tailored to meet your organization's unique requirements) or public courses (presented at a central training facility and open to students from any organization). These courses can also be presented online via webinar. For individuals who are Level 2 certified but wish to achieve a higher level of TOGAF® expertise, EA Principals also offers both Advanced Applied TOGAF and Advanced Applied ArchiMate training.

EA Principals also offers courses in the Department of Defense Architecture Framework (DoDAF) and the Federal/Federated Enterprise Architecture Framework (FEAF). Related training offered by EA Principals includes a range of diverse topics including Business Architecture, Business Analysis, Project Management, Knowledge Management, and Organizational Performance Assessment and Improvement.

Finally, EA Principals offers on-site assistance, coaching, and mentoring in all of the topics mentioned above. View the complete catalogue of offerings at www.eaprincipals.com.

TOGAF 9.2 Level 1 Volume 1 Test 1

Questions

1. The six parts of TOGAF include all of the following except:
   A. Part I: Introduction
   B. Part II: Architecture Development Method (ADM)
   C. Part III: ADM Guidelines and Techniques
   D. Part IV: Architecture Content Framework
   E. Part V: Enterprise Continuum and Tools
   F. Part VI: Architecture Capability Framework
   G. All of the above are parts of TOGAF

2. Guidelines, templates, patterns, and other forms of reference material that can be leveraged in order to accelerate the creation of new architectures for the enterprise are provided by.
   A. The Architecture Metamodel
   B. The Architecture Landscape
   C. The Reference Library
   D. The Standards Information Base

3. Performing initial implementation planning is a key activity of
   A. The Preliminary Phase
   B. Phase A
   C. Phase D
   D. Phase E

4. Assessing the dependencies, costs, and benefits of the various migration projects are activities in.
   A. Requirements Management
   B. Phase F
   C. Phase G
   D. Phase H

5. Governing and managing an Architecture Contract is a key activity of Phase F.
   A. True
   B. False

6. The primary purpose of connecting the Architecture Continuum to the Solutions Continuum is building Organization-Specific Solutions on
   A. Industry Solutions
   B. Common Systems Solutions
   C. Foundation Solutions
   D. All of the above

7. Objectives of Phase E include
   A. Generate the initial complete version of the Architecture Roadmap, based upon the gap analysis and candidate Architecture Roadmap components from Phases B, C, and D
   B. Determine whether an incremental approach is required, and if so identify Transition Architectures that will deliver continuous business value
   C. Define the overall Solution Building Blocks (SBBs) to finalize the Target Architecture based on the Architecture Building Blocks (ABBs)
   D. All of the above

8. Depending on the organization, principles may be established as any or all of the following except:
   A. Enterprise principles
   B. Information Systems principles
   C. IT principles
   D. Architecture principles

9. All of the following describe Building Blocks except:
   A. A Building Block is not re-usable
   B. Building Blocks can be combined with other building blocks
   C. Building Blocks can be defined at various levels of detail, depending on what stage of architecture development has been reached
   D. Building blocks can relate to "architectures" or "solutions."

10. The objectives of Phase B include
    A. Developing the Target Business Architecture that describes how the enterprise needs to operate to achieve the business goals, and respond to the strategic drivers set out in the Architecture Vision, in a way that addresses the Request for Architecture Work and stakeholder concerns
    B. Identifying candidate Architecture Roadmap components based upon gaps between the Baseline and Target Business Architectures
    C. A and B, above
    D. Neither A nor B, above

11. Categories of required architectural changes include all of the following except:
    A. Simplification change
    B. Incremental change
    C. Breakthrough change
    D. Re-architecting change

12. A good business scenario is
    A. Specific
    B. Measurable
    C. Actionable
    D. Realistic
    E. Time-bound
    F. All of the above

13. In TOGAF, a constituent of the architecture model that describes a single aspect of the overall model is referred to as
    A. An artifact
    B. A deliverable
    C. An Architecture Building Block (ABB)
    D. A view
    E. A viewpoint

14. Obtaining approval for a Statement of Architecture Work is an objective of
    A. The Preliminary Phase
    B. Phase A
    C. Phase B
    D. Requirements Management

15. Principles may be established as
    A. Enterprise principles
    B. IT principles
    C. Architecture principles
    D. Any or all of the above

16. Artifacts are generally classified as
    A. Catalogs (lists of things)
    B. Matrices (showing relationships between things)
    C. Diagrams (pictures of things)
    D. A and B, above
    E. A and C, above
    F. All of the above

17. Developing architectures in the Business, Application, Data, and Technology domains is an objective of all of the following except:
    A. Phase B, Business Architecture
    B. Phase C, Information Systems Architectures (Application & Data)
    C. Phase D, Technology Architecture
    D. Architecture Change Management

18. The objectives of Phase H include
    A. Formulating recommendations for each implementation project
    B. Ensure that the Enterprise Architecture Capability meets current requirements
    C. Ensure that the architecture lifecycle is maintained
    D. B and C, above

19. The phases of The Open Group Architecture Framework (TOGAF) include
    A. Preliminary Phase
    B. Phase A: Architecture Vision
    C. Phase B: Business Architecture
    D. Phase C: Information Systems Architectures
    E. Phase D: Technology Architecture
    F. Phase E: Opportunities and Solutions
    G. Phase F: Migration Planning
    H. Phase G: Implementation Governance
    I. Phase H: Architecture Change Management
    J. Requirements Management
    K. All of the above

20. The parameters, structures, and processes that support governance of the Architecture Repository are defined by
    A. The Architecture Landscape
    B. The Architecture Metamodel
    C. The Architecture Capability
    D. The Governance Log

21. The ADM supports the concept of iteration by all of the following except:
    A. Cycling around the Enterprise Continuum
    B. Cycling around the ADM
    C. Iterating between phases
    D. Cycling around a single phase

22. Key activities of Phase H include
    A. Ensuring that changes to the architecture are managed in a cohesive and architected way
    B. Providing flexibility to evolve rapidly in response to changes in the technology or business environment
    C. Monitoring the business and capacity management
    D. All of the above

23. A more granular architectural work product that describes an architecture from a specific viewpoint is.
    A. A building block
    B. An artifact
    C. A deliverable
    D. Any of the above
    E. None of the above

24. Typical examples of Stakeholders might include all of the following except:
    A. The Chief Architect
    B. An IT Project Team
    C. A Technology Supplier
    D. A government regulatory agency that is not related to the organization in question

25. The parameters, structures, and processes that support governance of the Architecture Repository are defined by the
    A. Governance Log
    B. Architecture Capability
    C. Reference Library
    D. Standards Information Base

26. Architecture domains supported by TOGAF include all of the following except:
    A. Business Architecture
    B. Strategic Architecture
    C. Data Architecture
    D. Application Architecture
    E. Technology Architecture

27. A representation of a subject of interest is
    A. An Enterprise Architecture
    B. An Architecture Model
    C. An Architecture
    D. A Framework

28. Regarding architectural views, all of the following are true except:
    A. A View provides methods for classifying architecture and solution artifacts
    B. A View is the representation of a related set of concerns
    C. A View is what is seen from a viewpoint
    D. A View may be represented by a model to demonstrate to stakeholders their areas of interest in the architecture

29. Typical providers of Common Systems Solutions include all of the following except:
    A. TOGAF Enterprise Architecture consultants
    B. Business process outsourcing vendors
    C. "Software as a service" vendors
    D. Computer systems vendors

30. What is an Architecture?
    A. A model of an organization showing its fundamental purpose for existing, its vision of its future state, its plans for achieving its vision, and core competencies needed to achieve the vision
    B. The fundamental concepts or properties of a system in its environment embodied in its elements, relationships, and in the principles of its design and evolution. (Source:
    C. ISO/IEC/IEEE 42010: 2011) The structure of components, their inter-relationships, and the principles and guidelines governing their design and evolution over time.
    D. All of the above
    E. B and C, above

31. A Stakeholder can be
    A. An individual
    B. A team
    C. An organization
    D. Any of the above

32. Architectures that guide the selection and integration of specific services from the Foundation Architecture to create an architecture useful for building common solutions across a wide number of relevant domains are referred to as
    A. Enterprise Architectures
    B. Common Systems Architectures
    C. Baseline Architectures
    D. Transition Architectures

33. Verifying and understanding the documented business strategy and goals is a concern of the activity in
    A. The Preliminary Phase
    B. Phase A
    C. Phase B
    D. Requirements Management

34. The discipline of monitoring, managing, and steering a business (or IS/IT landscape) to deliver the business outcome required is referred to as
    A. Strategic Planning
    B. Business Process Management
    C. Governance
    D. ITIL

35. A structuring of Architecture Building Blocks (ABBs) that are re-usable architecture assets is represented by
    A. The Architecture Content Framework
    B. The Architecture Landscape
    C. The Architecture Repository
    D. The Architecture Continuum

36. All of the following statements about a Common Systems Solution are true except:
    A. It consists of highly generic concepts, tools, products, services, and solution components
    B. It is an implementation of a Common Systems Architecture that is composed of a set of products and services, which may be certified or branded
    C. It represents the highest common denominator for one or more solutions in the industry segments that the Common Systems Solution supports
    D. It represents a collection of common requirements and capabilities, rather than those specific to a particular customer or industry

37. Steps involved in Phase A include
    A. Developing an Architecture Vision and value proposition to respond to the requirements and constraints
    B. Confirm and elaborate business goals, business drivers, and constraints
    C. Obtaining formal approval to proceed
    D. All of the above

38. Business Governance
    A. Ensures that the business processes and policies (and their operation) deliver the business outcomes
    B. Ensures that the business processes and policies (and their operation) adhere to relevant business regulation
    C. Both A and B, above
    D. Neither A nor B, above

39. Categories of solution in the Solutions Continuum include all of the following except:
    A. Foundation
    B. Common Systems
    C. Industry
    D. Enterprise-Specific

40. The main aspects of the approach taken in the Preliminary Phase include all of the following except:
    A. Selecting tools and techniques for viewpoints
    B. Defining the framework to be used
    C. Defining the relationships between management frameworks
    D. Evaluating the enterprise architecture's maturity

Test 1 Answers

1. The six parts of TOGAF include all of the following except: **H. All of the above are parts of TOGAF**   Open Group Standard TOGAF® Version 9.2, 1.1, pages 4-5
2. Guidelines, templates, patterns, and other forms of reference material that can be leveraged in order to accelerate the creation of new architectures for the enterprise are provided by.   **C. The Reference Library**   Open Group Standard TOGAF® Version 9.2, 2.7, page 17
3. Performing initial implementation planning is a key activity of   **D. Phase E**   N181 Reference Card Page 13 – Phase E under Steps
4. Assessing the dependencies, costs, and benefits of the various migration projects are activities in.   **B. Phase F**   N181 Reference Card Page 14 – Phase F under Steps
5. Governing and managing an Architecture Contract is a key activity of Phase F.   **B. False**   N181 Reference Card Page 11 – Phase G under Objectives
6. The primary purpose of connecting the Architecture Continuum to the Solutions Continuum is building Organization-Specific Solutions on   **D. All of the above**   Open Group Standard TOGAF® Version 9.2, 35.4.2, page 380
7. Objectives of Phase E include   **D. All of the above**   N181 Reference Card Page 13 – Phase E under Objectives and Steps

8. Depending on the organization, principles may be established as any or all of the following except:
B. Information Systems principles
Open Group Standard TOGAF® Version 9.2, 20.1, page 197
9. All of the following describe Building Blocks except:
A. A Building Block is not re-usable
Open Group Standard TOGAF® Version 9.2, 2.5, page 13
10. The objectives of Phase B include
C. A and B, above
N181 Reference Card Page 9 – Phase B under Objectives
11. Categories of required architectural changes include all of the following except:
C. Breakthrough change
Open Group Standard TOGAF® Version 9.2, 15.5.2, page 162
12. A good business scenario is
F. All of the above
TOGAF® Series Guide – Business Scenarios, pages 1-2
13. In TOGAF, a constituent of the architecture model that describes a single aspect of the overall model is referred to as
C. An Architecture Building Block (ABB)
Open Group Standard TOGAF® Version 9.2, 3.8, page 22
14. Obtaining approval for a Statement of Architecture Work is an objective of
B. Phase A
N181 Reference Card page 8, Phase A under Objectives
15. Principles may be established as
D. Any or all of the above
Open Group Standard TOGAF® Version 9.2, 20.1, page 197

16. Artifacts are generally classified as

F. All of the above

Open Group Standard TOGAF® Version 9.2, 2.5, page 13

---

17. Developing architectures in the Business, Application, Data, and Technology domains is an objective of all of the following except:

D. Architecture Change Management

N181 Reference Card ADM 9-12 under Steps

---

18. The objectives of Phase H include

D. B and C, above

N181 Reference Card Page 16 – Phase H under Objectives

---

19. The phases of The Open Group Architecture Framework (TOGAF) include

K. All of the above

Open Group Standard TOGAF® Version 9.2, 2.4, page 12

---

20. The parameters, structures, and processes that support governance of the Architecture Repository are defined by

C. The Architecture Capability

Open Group Standard TOGAF® Version 9.2, 2.7, page 16

---

21. The ADM supports the concept of iteration by all of the following except:

A. Cycling around the Enterprise Continuum

Open Group Standard TOGAF® Version 9.2, 18.2, page 180

---

22. Key activities of Phase H include

D. All of the above

N181 Reference Card Page 16 – Phase H under Objectives, Steps, and Outputs

---

23. A more granular architectural work product that describes an architecture from a specific viewpoint is.

B. An artifact

Open Group Standard TOGAF® Version 9.2, 2.5, page 13

might include all of the following except:

that is not related to the organization in question

sion 9.2, 21.3.1 page 214

rocesses that support governance of the Architecture Repository are

sion 9.2, 2.7, page 17

TOGAF include all of the following except:

B. Strategic Architecture

Open Group Standard TOGAF® Version 9.2, 4.5.4, page 47

27. A representation of a subject of interest is

B. An Architecture Model

Open Group Standard TOGAF® Version 9.2, 3.15, page 23

28. Regarding architectural views, all of the following are true except:

A. A View provides methods for classifying architecture and solution artifacts

Open Group Standard TOGAF® Version 9.2, 3.17, page 23

29. Typical providers of Common Systems Solutions include all of the following except:

A. TOGAF Enterprise Architecture consultants

Open Group Standard TOGAF® Version 9.2, 35.4.2, page 381

30. What is an Architecture?

E. B and C, above

Open Group Standard TOGAF® Version 9.2, 3.7, page 22

31. A Stakeholder can be

D. Any of the above

Open Group Standard TOGAF® Version 9.2, 3.72, page 31

32. Architectures that guide the selection and integration of specific services from the Foundation Architecture to create an architecture useful for building common solutions across a wide number of relevant domains are referred to as

B. Common Systems Architectures

Open Group Standard TOGAF® Version 9.2, 35.4.1, page 379

---

33. Verifying and understanding the documented business strategy and goals is a concern of the activity in

B. Phase A

Open Group Standard TOGAF® Version 9.2, 6.3.3, page 67

---

34. The discipline of monitoring, managing, and steering a business (or IS/IT landscape) to deliver the business outcome required is referred to as

C. Governance

Open Group Standard TOGAF® Version 9.2, 3.43, page 27

---

35. A structuring of Architecture Building Blocks (ABBs) that are re-usable architecture assets is represented by

D. The Architecture Continuum

Open Group Standard TOGAF® Version 9.2, 35.3, pages 376 - 377

---

36. All of the following statements about a Common Systems Solution are true except:

A. It consists of highly generic concepts, tools, products, services, and solution components

Open Group Standard TOGAF® Version 9.2, 35.4.2, page 381

---

37. Steps involved in Phase A include

D. All of the above

N181 Reference Card page 8, under Objectives

---

38. Business Governance

C. Both A and B, above

Open Group Standard TOGAF® Version 9.2, 3.27, page 25

39. Categories of solution in the Solutions Continuum include all of the following except:
D. Enterprise-Specific
Open Group Standard TOGAF® Version 9.2, 35.4.2, pages 380 - 381

40. The main aspects of the Preliminary Phase include all of the following except:
A. Selecting tools and techniques for viewpoints
Open Group Standard TOGAF® Version 9.2, 5.5, page 57

TOGAF 9.2 Level 1 Volume 1 Test 2

Questions

1. Providing continual monitoring and a change management process is a key activity of
   A. Phase E
   B. Phase F
   C. Phase G
   D. Phase H

2. In TOGAF, a view of the Architecture Repository that provides methods for classifying architecture and solution artifacts, both internal and external to the Architecture Repository, as they evolve from generic architectures to Organization-Specific Architectures, and similarly generic solutions to organization-specific solutions, is referred to as the
   A. Architecture Reference Model
   B. Architecture Content Framework
   C. Enterprise Continuum
   D. Architecture Continuum

3. Setting up a governance and support framework to provide business process and Architecture Governance through the ADM cycle is an objective of
   A. Phase A, Architecture Vision
   B. Phase G, Implementation Governance
   C. Requirements Management
   D. The Preliminary Phase

4. In order for the sponsor to identify the key decision makers and stakeholders and generate a Request for Architecture Work, which of the following requirements need to be articulated?
   A. Organization intents
   B. Strategic intent
   C. Forecast financial requirements
   D. Any one or more of the above

5. Governing and managing an Architecture Contract covering the overall implementation and deployment process is an objective of
   A. Phase E
   B. Phase F
   C. Phase G
   D. Phase H

6. Analyzing cost, benefits, and risk is an objective of.
   A. Preliminary Phase
   B. Phase E, Opportunities & Solutions
   C. Phase F, Migration Planning
   D. Phase H, Architecture Change Management

7. The main aspects of the Preliminary Phase include all of the following except:
   A. Defining the enterprise
   B. Defining the architecture principles that will inform any architecture work
   C. Analyzing the gaps between the Baseline and Target Architectures
   D. Evaluating the enterprise architecture's maturity

8. Finalizing the Architecture Vision and Architecture Definition Documents, in line with the agreed implementation approach, is an objective of
   A. Phase A
   B. Phase E
   C. Phase F
   D. Phase G

9. A good enterprise architecture can bring important business benefits, including all of the following except:
   A. Better alignment and integration of the organization's purpose, vision, and mission
   B. A more efficient IT operation
   C. Better return on existing investment
   D. Reduced risk for future investment

10. The main aspects of the Preliminary Phase include all of the following except:
    A. Understanding the business environment
    B. Analyzing the gaps between the Baseline and Target Architectures
    C. Ensuring high-level management commitment
    D. Obtaining agreement on scope

11. Key activities of Phase E include all of the following except:
    A. Identifying dependencies
    B. Assessing priorities
    C. Performing initial implementation planning
    D. Identifying stakeholders, their concerns, and objectives

12. Governing and managing an Architecture Contract is a key activity of
    A. Phase H
    B. Phase G
    C. Phase F
    D. Phase E

13. What are used to describe transitional Target Architectures necessary for effective realization of the Target Architecture?
    A. Baseline Architectures
    B. Phase Architectures
    C. Milestone Architectures
    D. Transition Architectures

14. The Architecture Landscape contains
    A. Strategic Architectures
    B. Segment Architectures
    C. Capability Architectures
    D. All of the above

15. Ensuring that the Implementation and Migration Plan is coordinated with the various management frameworks in use within the enterprise is an objective of
    A. Phase F
    B. Phase G
    C. Phase H
    D. Requirements Management

16. In the TOGAF Template for Defining Principles, all of the following are true except:
    A. The "Name" element should represent both the essence of the rule and be easy to remember
    B. The "Statement" element should succinctly and unambiguously communicate the fundamental rule
    C. The "Rationale" element should highlight the business benefits of adhering to the principle, using business terminology
    D. The "Impact" element should highlight the requirements, both for the business and IT, for carrying out the principle – in terms of resources, costs, and activities/tasks

17. A Capability is an ability that can be possessed by
    A. An organization
    B. A person
    C. A system
    D. Any of the above

18. Building blocks can be defined at various levels of detail and can be categorized as Architecture Building Blocks (ABBs) and Solution Building Blocks (SBBs).
    A. True
    B. False

19. Resources suggested by TOGAF for requirements management include
    A. Business Scenarios
    B. Volere requirements tools
    C. Both A and B, above
    D. Neither A nor B, above; TOGAF does not suggest specific resources for requirements management

20. The purpose of Enterprise Continuum is primarily
    A. To provide artifact repositories
    B. To define taxonomies
    C. To aid communication
    D. To establish a continuum of generic to specific building blocks

21. A Building Block
    A. Is a (potentially re-usable) component of business, IT, or architectural capability
    B. Can be defined at various levels of detail, depending on what stage of architecture development has been reached
    C. Can relate to "architectures" or "solutions."
    D. All of the above

22. The TOGAF phase that describes the development of a Business Architecture to support an agreed Architecture Vision is Phase A: Architecture Vision.
    A. True
    B. False

23. In the TOGAF Template for Defining Principles, all of the following are true except:
    A. The "Name" element should represent both the essence of the rule and be easy to remember
    B. The "Description" element should succinctly and unambiguously communicate the fundamental rule
    C. The "Rationale" element should highlight the business benefits of adhering to the principle, using business terminology
    D. The "Implication" element should highlight the requirements, both for the business and IT, for carrying out the principle – in terms of resources, costs, and activities/tasks

24. An architectural view of the building blocks that are in use within the organization today is called.
    A. The Architecture Continuum
    B. The Architecture Landscape
    C. The Architecture Metamodel
    D. None of the above

25. Objectives of Phase G, Implementation Governance, include all of the following except:
    A. Analyzing cost, benefits, and risk
    B. Provide architectural oversight for the implementation
    C. Prepare and issue Architecture Contracts
    D. Ensure that the implementation project conforms to the architecture

26. Identifying and scoping the elements of the enterprise organizations affected and defining the constraints and assumptions is an objective of the Preliminary Phase.
    A. True
    B. False

27. A work product that is contractually specified and in turn formally reviewed, agreed, and signed off by the stakeholders is referred to as a (an).
    A. Deliverable
    B. Artifact
    C. Building block
    D. All of the above
    E. None of the above

28. An Architecture Vision is
    A. A high-level, aspirational view of the Target Architecture
    B. A phase in the ADM which delivers understanding and definition of the Architecture Vision
    C. A specific deliverable describing the Architecture Vision
    D. All of the above

29. Phases B, C, and D develop architectures in which domains?
    A. Business, Information Systems, and Technology
    B. Business, Information Systems, Security, and Technology
    C. Information Systems, Security, and Technology
    D. Business, Application, and Data

30. Industry Solutions cannot be tailored to an individual organization's requirements.
    A. True
    B. False

31. The major components within an Architecture Repository include all of the following except:
    A. The Architecture Metamodel
    B. The TOGAF Reference Model
    C. The Architecture Capability
    D. The Architecture Landscape
    E. The Standards Information Base (SIB)
    F. The Reference Library
    G. The Governance Log

32. Regarding architectural views, all of the following are true except:
    A. A View is the representation of a related set of concerns
    B. A View is what is seen from a viewpoint
    C. A View may be represented by a model to demonstrate to stakeholders their areas of interest in the architecture
    D. A View must be visual or graphical in nature

33. The Architecture Landscape is divided into all of the following except:
    A. Strategic Architectures
    B. Transition Architectures
    C. Segment Architectures
    D. Capability Architectures

34. The Architecture Metamodel describes the organizationally tailored application of an architecture framework, including a metamodel for architecture content.
    A. True
    B. False

35. A Solution Architecture
    A. Typically applies to a single project or project release
    B. Assists in the translation of requirements into a solution vision, high-level business, and/or IT system specifications
    C. Typically applies to a portfolio of implementation tasks
    D. All of the above

36. Objectives of Phase A, Architecture Vision, include all of the following except:
    A. Create the Architecture Vision
    B. Undertake the preparation and initiation activities required to meet the business directive for a new enterprise architecture
    C. Validate the business context and create the Statement of Architecture Work
    D. Obtain approvals

37. At a high level, classes of architectural information that are expected to be held within an Architecture Repository include all of the following except:
    A. The Architecture Metamodel
    B. The Architecture Capability
    C. The Architecture Principles
    D. The Architecture Landscape

38. Phase E: Opportunities and Solutions conducts initial implementation planning and the identification of delivery vehicles for the architecture defined in the previous phases.
    A. True
    B. False

39. A Transition Architecture
    A. Is a formal description of the enterprise architecture showing periods of transition and development for particular parts of the enterprise
    B. Is used to provide an overview of current and target capability
    C. Ensures that the implementation project conforms to the architecture
    D. A and B, above
    E. All of the above

40. All of the following statements about a Common Systems Solution are true except:
    A. It is an implementation of a Common Systems Architecture that is composed of a set of products and services, which may be certified or branded
    B. It consists of highly generic concepts, tools, products, services, and solution components
    C. It represents the highest common denominator for one or more solutions in the industry segments that the Common Systems Solution supports
    D. It represents a collection of common requirements and capabilities, rather than those specific to a particular customer or industry

Test 2 Answers

1. Providing continual monitoring and a change management process is a key activity of **D. Phase H** N181 Reference Card Page 16 – Phase H under Steps
2. In TOGAF, a view of the Architecture Repository that provides methods for classifying architecture and solution artifacts, both internal and external to the Architecture Repository, as they evolve from generic architectures to Organization-Specific Architectures, and similarly generic solutions to organization-specific solutions, is referred to as the **C. Enterprise Continuum** Open Group Standard TOGAF® Version 9.2, 35.1, page 375
3. Setting up a governance and support framework to provide business process and Architecture Governance through the ADM cycle is an objective of **D. The Preliminary Phase** Open Group Standard TOGAF® Version 9.2, 5.1, page 52
4. In order for the sponsor to identify the key decision makers and stakeholders and generate a Request for Architecture Work, which of the following requirements need to be articulated? **D. Any one or more of the above** Open Group Standard TOGAF® Version 9.2, 5.5.2-5.5.3, pages 58-59
5. Governing and managing an Architecture Contract covering the overall implementation and deployment process is an objective of **C. Phase G** N181 Reference Card Page 15 – Phase G under Objectives
6. Analyzing cost, benefits, and risk is an objective of. **C. Phase F, Migration Planning** N181 Reference Card Page 14 – Phase F under Steps

7. The main aspects of the Preliminary Phase include all of the following except:

C. Analyzing the gaps between the Baseline and Target Architectures

Open Group Standard TOGAF® Version 9.2, 5.1, page 52

---

8. Finalizing the Architecture Vision and Architecture Definition Documents, in line with the agreed implementation approach, is an objective of

C. Phase F

N181 Reference Card Page 14 – Phase F under Objectives

---

9. A good enterprise architecture can bring important business benefits, including all of the following except:

A. Better alignment and integration of the organization's purpose, vision, and mission

Open Group Standard TOGAF® Version 9.2, 1.3, page 7

---

10. The main aspects of the Preliminary Phase include all of the following except:

B. Analyzing the gaps between the Baseline and Target Architectures

Open Group Standard TOGAF® Version 9.2, 5.1, page 52

---

11. Key activities of Phase E include all of the following except:

D. Identifying stakeholders, their concerns, and objectives

N181 Reference Card Page 13 – Phase E under Objectives and Steps

---

12. Governing and managing an Architecture Contract is a key activity of

B. Phase G

N181 Reference Card Page 15 – Phase G under Objectives

---

13. What are used to describe transitional Target Architectures necessary for effective realization of the Target Architecture?

D. Transition Architectures

Open Group Standard TOGAF® Version 9.2, 32.2.3 page 352

14. The Architecture Landscape contains **D. All of the above** Open Group Standard TOGAF® Version 9.2, 37.2, page 392
15. Ensuring that the Implementation and Migration Plan is coordinated with the various management frameworks in use within the enterprise is an objective of **A. Phase F** N181 Reference Card Page 14 – Phase F under Objectives
16. In the TOGAF Template for Defining Principles, all of the following are true except: **D. The "Impact" element should highlight the requirements, both for the business and IT, for carrying out the principle – in terms of resources, costs, and activities/tasks** Open Group Standard TOGAF® Version 9.2, 20.3, page 198
17. A Capability is an ability that can be possessed by **D. Any of the above** Open Group Standard TOGAF® Version 9.2, 3.30, page 25
18. Building blocks can be defined at various levels of detail and can be categorized as Architecture Building Blocks (ABBs) and Solution Building Blocks (SBBs). **A. True** Open Group Standard TOGAF® Version 9.2, 3.23, page 24
19. Resources suggested by TOGAF for requirements management include **C. Both A and B, above** Open Group Standard TOGAF® Version 9.2, 16.5.3, page 172
20. The purpose of Enterprise Continuum is primarily **C. To aid communication** Open Group Standard TOGAF® Version 9.2, 35.1 page 375

21. A Building Block

D. All of the above

Open Group Standard TOGAF® Version 9.2, 3.23, page 24

22. The TOGAF phase that describes the development of a Business Architecture to support an agreed Architecture Vision is Phase A: Architecture Vision.

B. False

Open Group Standard TOGAF® Version 9.2, 2.4, page 12

23. In the TOGAF Template for Defining Principles, all of the following are true except:

B. The "Description" element should succinctly and unambiguously communicate the fundamental rule

Open Group Standard TOGAF® Version 9.2, 23.2, page 236

24. An architectural view of the building blocks that are in use within the organization today is called.

B. The Architecture Landscape

Open Group Standard TOGAF® Version 9.2, 2.7, page 17

25. Objectives of Phase G, Implementation Governance, include all of the following except:

A. Analyzing cost, benefits, and risk

N181 Reference Card Page 15 – Phase G under Objectives

26. Identifying and scoping the elements of the enterprise organizations affected and defining the constraints and assumptions is an objective of the Preliminary Phase.

A. True

Open Group Standard TOGAF® Version 9.2, 5.1, page 52

27. A work product that is contractually specified and in turn formally reviewed, agreed, and signed off by the stakeholders is referred to as a (an).

A. Deliverable

Open Group Standard TOGAF® Version 9.2, 3.37, page 26

28. An Architecture Vision is
D. All of the above
Open Group Standard TOGAF® Version 9.2, 3.19, page 24
29. Phases B, C, and D develop architectures in which domains?
A. Business, Information Systems, and Technology
N181 Reference Card ADM Pages 9 - 12 under Steps
30. Industry Solutions cannot be tailored to an individual organization's requirements.
B. False
Open Group Standard TOGAF® Version 9.2, 35.4.2, page 382
31. The major components within an Architecture Repository include all of the following except:
B. The TOGAF Reference Model
Open Group Standard TOGAF® Version 9.2, 2.7, page 16
32. Regarding architectural views, all of the following are true except:
D. A View must be visual or graphical in nature
Open Group Standard TOGAF® Version 9.2, 3.17, page 23
33. The Architecture Landscape is divided into all of the following except:
B. Transition Architectures
Open Group Standard TOGAF® Version 9.2, 37.2, page 392
34. The Architecture Metamodel describes the organizationally tailored application of an architecture framework, including a metamodel for architecture content.
A. True
Open Group Standard TOGAF® Version 9.2, 2.7, page 17
35. A Solution Architecture
D. All of the above
Open Group Standard TOGAF® Version 9.2, 3.69, page 31

EA PRINCIPALS 400 TOGAF® 9.2 FOUNDATION LEVEL 1 PRACTICE QUESTIONS VOL 1

36. Objectives of Phase A, Architecture Vision, include all of the following except: **B. Undertake the preparation and initiation activities required to meet the business directive for a new enterprise architecture** N181 Reference Card Page 8, Phase A under Objectives
37. At a high level, classes of architectural information that are expected to be held within an Architecture Repository include all of the following except: **C. The Architecture Principles** Open Group Standard TOGAF® Version 9.2, 37.1, page 391
38. Phase E: Opportunities and Solutions conducts initial implementation planning and the identification of delivery vehicles for the architecture defined in the previous phases. **A. True** Open Group Standard TOGAF® Version 9.2, 2.4, page 12
39. A Transition Architecture **D. A and B, above** Open Group Standard TOGAF® Version 9.2, 3.80, page 33
40. All of the following statements about a Common Systems Solution are true except: **B. It consists of highly generic concepts, tools, products, services, and solution components** Open Group Standard TOGAF® Version 9.2, 35.4.2, page 381

TOGAF 9.2 Level 1 Volume 1 Test 3

Questions

1. The Business Architecture is often necessary as a means of
   A. Demonstrating the business value of subsequent architecture work to key stakeholders
   B. Demonstrating the return on investment to key stakeholders from supporting and participating in the subsequent work
   C. Both A and B, above
   D. Neither A and B, above

2. Selecting and implementing supporting tools and other infrastructure to support the architecture activity is an objective of the Preliminary Phase.
   A. True
   B. False

3. The four categories of solution in the Solutions Continuum are
   A. Strategic, Common Systems, Industry, Organization-Specific
   B. Foundation, Common Systems, Industry, Organization-Specific
   C. Foundation, General Systems, Industry, Organization-Specific
   D. Foundation, Common Systems, Business Sector, Organization-Specific
   E. Foundation, Common Systems, Industry, Enterprise-Specific

4. In TOGAF, an implementation of an Industry Architecture that provides re-usable packages of common components and services specific to an industry is referred to as
   A. A Foundation Solution
   B. A Common Systems Solution
   C. An Industry Solution
   D. An Organization-Specific Solution

5. Obtaining formal approval to proceed is an objective of
   A. The Preliminary Phase
   B. Requirements Management
   C. Phase A
   D. All phases of the TOGAF ADM

6. The organizationally tailored application of an architecture framework, including a method for architecture development and a metamodel for architecture content, is described in the Architecture Capability.
   A. True
   B. False

7. Programming languages, operating systems, foundational data structures (such as EDIFACT), generic approaches to organization structuring, and foundational structures for organizing IT operations (such as ITIL) are examples of
   A. Foundation Solutions
   B. Common Systems Solutions
   C. Industry Solutions
   D. Organization-Specific Solutions

8. In order for the sponsor to identify the key decision makers and stakeholders and generate a Request for Architecture Work, which of the following requirements need to be articulated?
   A. Business requirements
   B. Cultural aspirations
   C. Organization intents
   D. Any one or more of the above

9. Ensuring that the Enterprise Architecture Capability meets current requirements is an objective of:
   A. Phase H
   B. Phase G
   C. Phase F
   D. Phase E

10. The standards with which new architectures must comply, which may include industry standards, selected products and services from suppliers, or shared services already deployed within the organization, are captured by the Architecture Repository.
    A. True
    B. False

11. The main aspects of the Preliminary Phase include
    A. Defining the framework to be used
    B. Defining the relationships between management frameworks
    C. Evaluating the enterprise architecture's maturity
    D. All of the above

12. Obtaining approval for a Statement of Architecture Work that defines a program of works to develop and deploy the architecture outlined in the Architecture Vision is an objective of:
    A. The Preliminary Phase
    B. Phase A
    C. Phase E
    D. Requirements Management

13. Key activities of Phase H include
    A. Identify deployment resources and skills
    B. Provide analysis for architecture change management
    C. Manage governance process
    D. B and C, above

14. An architectural oversight of the implementation is provided in Phase A: Architecture Vision.
    A. True
    B. False

15. Specific areas to consider in the organizational context, identified in the Preliminary Phase, include
    A. The intentions and culture of the organization
    B. The stakeholders
    C. The commercial models and budget for the enterprise architecture
    D. All of the above

16. Monitoring implementation work for conformance is a key activity of:
    A. Phase G
    B. Phase H
    C. Phase E
    D. Phase F

17. Articulating an Architecture Vision and value proposition to respond to the requirements and constraints is an objective of
    A. Requirements Management
    B. Phase B
    C. Phase A
    D. The Preliminary Phase

18. Defining the requirements for architecture work is one of the main aspects of Phase A, Architecture Vision.
    A. True
    B. False

19. Deriving a series of Transition Architectures that deliver continuous business value (e.g., capability increments) through the exploitation of opportunities to realize the building blocks is an objective of
    A. Phase B
    B. Phase E
    C. Phase F
    D. Phase H

20. Ensuring conformance of the deployed solution with the Target Architecture is an objective of
    A. Phase H
    B. Phase G
    C. Phase F
    D. Phase E

21. The six parts of TOGAF include all of the following except:
    A. Part I: Introduction
    B. Part II: Architecture Development Method (ADM)
    C. Part III: ADM Guidelines and Techniques
    D. Part VII: Service Oriented Architecture

22. Guidelines, templates, patterns, and other forms of reference material that can be leveraged in order to accelerate the creation of new architectures for the enterprise are provided by the Reference Library.
    A. True
    B. False

23. Key Steps of Phase G include
    A. Perform enterprise architecture compliance reviews
    B. Guide development of solutions deployment
    C. Perform post-implementation review and close the implementation
    D. All of the above

24. Industry reference models are examples of
    A. Vertical models of architecture frameworks
    B. External architecture and solution artifacts
    C. Primary resources for SBBs
    D. Secondary architecture landscape repository resources

25. In TOGAF, a Deliverable is
    A. Contractually specified
    B. Formally reviewed, agreed, and signed off by the stakeholders
    C. A and B, above
    D. Neither A nor B, above

26. A set of reference materials and guidelines for establishing an architecture function or capability within an organization is an Architecture Content Framework.
    A. True
    B. False

27. Architecture principles can be divided into:
    A. Architecture principles define the underlying general rules and guidelines for the use and deployment of all IT resources and assets across the enterprise.
    B. Architecture principles reflect a level of consensus among the various elements of the enterprise and form the basis for making future IT decisions.
    C. Architecture principles need not be clearly related back to the business objectives and key architecture drivers.
    D. All of the above
    E. A and B, above

28. The six parts of TOGAF include all of the following except:
    A. Part IV: Architecture Content Framework
    B. Part V: Enterprise Continuum and Tools
    C. Part VI: TOGAF Reference Models
    D. Part VI: Architecture Capability Framework

29. Key Steps in Phase B, Business Architecture include:
    A. Select reference models, viewpoints, and tools
    B. Conduct formal stakeholder review
    C. Define candidate roadmap components
    D. All of the above

30. The process of managing architecture requirements throughout the ADM is examined in Phase E: Opportunities and Solutions.
    A. True
    B. False

31. Which of these answers is one of the descriptions of an architecture framework?
    A. A framework is a high-level method and a set of supporting tools
    B. An architecture framework is a method for developing a foundational structure and for supporting the development of other frameworks.
    C. It uses the concepts of Building Blocks, which are discrete tools for creating an architecture but are not re-useable in some form in creating future architectures.
    D. All of the above describe an architecture framework.

32. An Architecture Vision is all of the following except:
    A. A high-level, aspirational view of the Target Architecture
    B. A specification that has been formally reviewed and agreed upon
    C. A phase in the ADM which delivers understanding and definition of the Architecture Vision
    D. A specific deliverable describing the Architecture Vision

33. Most reasons to constrain (or restrict) the scope of the architectural activity to be undertaken relate to limits in all of the following except:
    A. The organizational authority of the team producing the architecture
    B. The objectives and stakeholder concerns to be addressed within the architecture
    C. The effectiveness of the Security Architecture
    D. The availability of people, finance, and other resources

34. Evaluating the enterprise architecture's maturity is one of the main aspects of the Preliminary Phase.
    A. True
    B. False

35. The Enterprise Continuum comprises several complementary concepts:
    A. The Architecture Continuum
    B. The Solutions Continuum
    C. The Business Continuum
    D. All of the above
    E. A and B, above

36. In TOGAF, the business strategy, governance, organization, and key business processes information, as well as the interaction between these concepts is referred to as.
    A. Foundation Architecture
    B. Baseline Architecture
    C. Business Architecture
    D. Business Foundation

37. Performing initial implementation planning, identifying delivery vehicles for the building blocks identified in the previous phases, and identifying major implementation projects and grouping them into Transition Architectures are objectives of
    A. Phase A, Architecture Vision
    B. Phase E, Opportunities and Solutions
    C. Phase F, Migration Planning
    D. Phase H, Architecture Change Management

38. Strategic Architectures provide an organizing framework for operational and change activity and allow for direction setting at an executive level
    A. True
    B. False

39. A set of reference materials and guidelines for establishing an architecture function or capability within an organization is.
    A. The Enterprise Continuum and Tools
    B. The ADM Guidelines and Techniques
    C. An Architecture Capability Framework
    D. An Architecture Repository

40. Objectives of Phase A, Architecture Vision, include all of the following except:
    A. Set the scope, constraints, and expectations for a TOGAF project
    B. Validate the business context and create the Statement of Architecture Work
    C. Identify major implementation projects, and grouping them into Transition Architectures
    D. Obtain approvals

Test 3 Answers

1. The Business Architecture is often necessary as a means of **C. Both A and B, above** Open Group Standard TOGAF® Version 9.2, 7.5.1, page 88
2. Selecting and implementing supporting tools and other infrastructure to support the architecture activity is an objective of the Preliminary Phase. **A. True** Open Group Standard TOGAF® Version 9.2, 5.1, page 52
3. The four categories of solution in the Solutions Continuum are **B. Foundation, Common Systems, Industry, Organization-Specific** Open Group Standard TOGAF® Version 9.2, 35.4.2, page 381
4. In TOGAF, an implementation of an Industry Architecture that provides re-usable packages of common components and services specific to an industry is referred to as **C. An Industry Solution** Open Group Standard TOGAF® Version 9.2, 35.4.2, page 382
5. Obtaining formal approval to proceed is an objective of **C. Phase A** N181 Reference Card page 8, Phase A under Objectives
6. The organizationally tailored application of an architecture framework, including a method for architecture development and a metamodel for architecture content, is described in the Architecture Capability. **B. False (This is the definition for the Architecture Metamodel)** Open Group Standard TOGAF® Version 9.2, 37.1, page 391
7. Programming languages, operating systems, foundational data structures (such as EDIFACT), generic approaches to organization structuring, and foundational structures for organizing IT operations (such as ITIL) are examples of **A. Foundation Solutions** Open Group Standard TOGAF® Version 9.2, 35.4.2, page 381

8. In order for the sponsor to identify the key decision makers and stakeholders and generate a Request for Architecture Work, which of the following requirements need to be articulated?

D. Any one or more of the above

Open Group Standard TOGAF® Version 9.2, 32.2.17, page 362

9. Ensuring that the Enterprise Architecture Capability meets current requirements is an objective of:

A. Phase H

N181 Reference Card Page 16 – Phase H under Objectives

10. The standards with which new architectures must comply, which may include industry standards, selected products and services from suppliers, or shared services already deployed within the organization, are captured by the Architecture Repository.

B. False

Open Group Standard TOGAF® Version 9.2, 2.7, page 16

11. The main aspects of the Preliminary Phase include

D. All of the above

Open Group Standard TOGAF® Version 9.2, 5.1, page 52

12. Obtaining approval for a Statement of Architecture Work that defines a program of works to develop and deploy the architecture outlined in the Architecture Vision is an objective of:

B. Phase A

N181 Reference Card page 8, Phase A under Objectives

13. Key activities of Phase H include

D. B and C, above

N181 Reference Card Page 16 – Phase H under Objectives

14. An architectural oversight of the implementation is provided in Phase A: Architecture Vision.

B. False

Open Group Standard TOGAF® Version 9.2, 2.4, page 12

15. Specific areas to consider in the organizational context, identified in the Preliminary Phase, include

D. All of the above

Open Group Standard TOGAF® Version 9.2, 5.5.2, page 58

---

16. Monitoring implementation work for conformance is a key activity of

A. Phase G

N181 Reference Card Page 15 – Phase G under Objectives

---

17. Articulating an Architecture Vision and value proposition to respond to the requirements and constraints is an objective of

C. Phase A

N181 Reference Card page 8, Phase A under Objectives

---

18. Defining the requirements for architecture work is one of the main aspects of Phase A, Architecture Vision.

B. False

Open Group Standard TOGAF® Version 9.2, 5.5, page 57

---

19. Deriving a series of Transition Architectures that deliver continuous business value (e.g., capability increments) through the exploitation of opportunities to realize the building blocks is an objective of

B. Phase E

N181 Reference Card Page 13 – Phase E under Objectives

---

20. Ensuring conformance of the deployed solution with the Target Architecture is an objective of

B. Phase G

N181 Reference Card Page 15 – Phase G under Steps and Objectives

---

21. The six parts of TOGAF include all of the following except:

D. Part VII: Service Oriented Architecture

Open Group Standard TOGAF® Version 9.2, 1.1, pages 4-5

22. Guidelines, templates, patterns, and other forms of reference material that can be leveraged in order to accelerate the creation of new architectures for the enterprise are provided by the Reference Library.

A. True

Open Group Standard TOGAF® Version 9.2, 37.1, page 391

23. Key activities of Phase G include

D. All of the above

N181 Reference Card Page 15 – Phase G under Steps

24. Industry reference models are examples of

B. External architecture and solution artifacts

Open Group Standard TOGAF® Version 9.2, 35 .2 page 375

25. In TOGAF, a Deliverable is

C. A and B, above

Open Group Standard TOGAF® Version 9.2, 3.37, page 26

26. A set of reference materials and guidelines for establishing an architecture function or capability within an organization is an Architecture Content Framework.

B. False

Open Group Standard TOGAF® Version 9.2, 29.1, page 271

27. Architecture principles can be divided into:

E. A and B, above

Open Group Standard TOGAF® Version 9.2, 20.2, page 198

28. The six parts of TOGAF include all of the following except:

C. Part VI: TOGAF Reference Models

Open Group Standard TOGAF® Version 9.2, 1.1, pages 4-5

29. Key Steps in Phase B, Business Architecture include:

D. All of the Above

Open Group Standard TOGAF® Version 9.2, 7.3, page 80

30. The process of managing architecture requirements throughout the ADM is examined in Phase E: Opportunities and Solutions.

B. False

Open Group Standard TOGAF® Version 9.2, 2.4, page 12

---

31. Which of these answers is one of the descriptions of an architecture framework?

A. An architecture framework is a method for developing a foundational structure and for supporting the development of other frameworks.

Open Group Standard TOGAF® Version 9.2, 1.3 page 8

---

32. An Architecture Vision is all of the following except:

B. A specification that has been formally reviewed and agreed upon

Open Group Standard TOGAF® Version 9.2, 3.19, page 24

---

33. Most reasons to constrain (or restrict) the scope of the architectural activity to be undertaken relate to limits in all of the following except:

C. The effectiveness of the Security Architecture

Open Group Standard TOGAF® Version 9.2, 4.5, 44

---

34. Evaluating the enterprise architecture's maturity is one of the main aspects of the Preliminary Phase.

A. True

Open Group Standard TOGAF® Version 9.2, 5.2.3, page 53

---

35. The Enterprise Continuum comprises several complementary concepts:

E. A and B, above

Open Group Standard TOGAF® Version 9.2, 2.6, page 15

---

36. In TOGAF, the business strategy, governance, organization, and key business processes information, as well as the interaction between these concepts is referred to as.

C. Business Architecture

Open Group Standard TOGAF® Version 9.2, 3.24, page 24

37. Performing initial implementation planning, identifying delivery vehicles for the building blocks identified in the previous phases, and identifying major implementation projects and grouping them into Transition Architectures are objectives of

B. Phase E, Opportunities and Solutions

N181 Reference Card Page 13 – Phase E under Objectives

---

38. Strategic Architectures provide an organizing framework for operational and change activity and allow for direction setting at an executive level

A. True

Open Group Standard TOGAF® Version 9.2, 37.2, page 392

---

39. A set of reference materials and guidelines for establishing an architecture function or capability within an organization is.

C. An Architecture Capability Framework

Open Group Standard TOGAF® Version 9.2, 39.1, page 405

---

40. Objectives of Phase A, Architecture Vision, include all of the following except:

C. Identify major implementation projects, and grouping them into Transition Architectures

N181 Reference Card ADM Page 8, Phase A under Objectives

TOGAF 9.2 Level 1 Volume 1 Test 4

Questions

1. The main aspects of the Preliminary Phase include all of the following except:
   A. Establishing principles
   B. Establishing governance structure
   C. Agreeing on the architecture method to be adopted
   D. Developing a Target Business Architecture

2. Applications use data and are supported by multiple technology components and are therefore part of the Technology Architecture.
   A. True
   B. False

3. The description of a future state of the architecture being developed for an organization is referred to as the.
   A. Architecture Vision
   B. Target Architecture
   C. Strategic Architecture
   D. None of the above

4. 670. The objectives of Phase E, Opportunities and Solutions, include all of the following except:
   A. Perform initial implementation planning
   B. Identify of delivery vehicles for the building blocks identified in the previous phases
   C. Analyzing gaps
   D. Group major implementation projects into Transition Architectures

5. Types of reference material provided by the Reference Library include all of the following except:
   A. Guidelines
   B. Templates
   C. Selected products and services from suppliers
   D. Patterns

6. Examples of artifacts include a network diagram, a server specification, a use-case specification, a list of architectural requirements, and a business interaction matrix.
   A. True
   B. False

7. All of the following statements about Viewpoints are true except:
   A. A definition of the perspective from which a view is taken
   B. A specification of the conventions for constructing and using a view
   C. A View must be visual or graphical in nature
   D. The vantage point or perspective that determines what you see

8. Examples of Industry Solutions include
   A. A physical database schema
   B. An industry-specific point-of-service device
   C. Both A and B, above
   D. Neither A nor B, above

9. Grouping projects into Transition Architectures is a key activity of
   A. Phase A
   B. Phase E
   C. Phase D
   D. The Preliminary Phase

10. Project establishment and initiating an iteration of the Architecture Development Cycle – setting the scope, constraints, and expectations for the iteration – is the purpose of the Preliminary Phase.
    A. True
    B. False

11. Examples of Common Systems Architectures include all of the following except:
    A. Security Architecture
    B. Management Architecture
    C. Network Architecture
    D. Foundation Architecture

12. Types of reference material provided by the Reference Library include all of the following except:
    A. Guidelines
    B. Templates
    C. Patterns
    D. Shared services already deployed within the organization

13. The objectives of Phase B include all of the following except:
    A. Developing the Target Business Architecture that describes how the enterprise needs to operate to achieve the business goals, and respond to the strategic drivers set out in the Architecture Vision, in a way that addresses the Request for Architecture Work and stakeholder concerns
    B. Identifying candidate Architecture Roadmap components based upon gaps between the Baseline and Target Business Architectures
    C. Validating business principles, goals, drivers, and Key Performance Indicators (KPIs)

14. An organization is prepared to undertake successful enterprise architecture projects by the Preliminary Phase.
    A. True
    B. False

15. An enterprise management system product and a security system product are examples of.
    A. Organization-Specific Solutions
    B. Industry Solutions
    C. Common Systems Solutions
    D. Foundation Solutions

16. Develop a high-level aspirational vision of the capabilities and business value to be delivered as a result of the proposed Enterprise Architecture is an objective of:
    A. The Preliminary Phase
    B. Phase A, Architecture Vision
    C. Phase B, Business Architecture
    D. Requirements Management

17. Required architectural changes that can normally be handled via change management techniques are referred to as
    A. Simplification change
    B. Incremental change
    C. Re-architecting change
    D. Transactional change

18. Deliverables represent
    A. The output of projects and those deliverables that are in documentation form that will typically be archived at completion of a project
    B. The output of projects that will be transitioned into an Architecture Repository as a reference model, standard, or snapshot of the Architecture Landscape at a point in time
    C. Neither A nor B, above
    D. Both A and B, above

19. Defining the framework to be used is one of the main aspects of
    A. Phase A, Architecture Vision
    B. Phase B, Business Architecture
    C. The Preliminary Phase
    D. Requirements Management

20. Once an Architecture Vision is defined and documented in the Statement of Architecture Work, it is critical to use the Architecture Vision to build a consensus, because
    A. Without this consensus it is very unlikely that a Business Capability assessment will be accomplished
    B. Without this consensus it is very unlikely that the final architecture will be accepted by the organization as a whole
    C. Without this consensus it is very unlikely that a Business Transformation Readiness Assessment will be accomplished
    D. Without this consensus it is very unlikely that a Capability Maturity Model will be developed

21. The objectives of Phase H include
    A. Assessing the performance of the architecture and making recommendations for change
    B. Establishing an architecture change management process for the new enterprise architecture baseline that is achieved with completion of Phase G
    C. Operating the Governance Framework
    D. All of the above

22. The major components within an Architecture Repository include all of the following except:
    A. The Architecture Metamodel
    B. The Architecture Capability
    C. The Architecture Landscape
    D. The Standards Information Base (SIB)
    E. The Reference Library
    F. The Governance Log
    G. All of the above are components of an Architecture Repository

23. A useful way of assessing the ability of an enterprise to exercise different capabilities is through the use of
    A. Total Quality Management (TQM)
    B. Capability Maturity Models (CMMs)
    C. Lean/Six-Sigma
    D. Any of the above

24. Ensuring conformance with the Target Architecture by implementation projects is an objective of:
    A. Phase G
    B. Phase H
    C. Phase E
    D. Phase F

25. The initial phase of an Architecture Development Cycle, which includes information about defining the scope, identifying the stakeholders, creating the Architecture Vision, and obtaining approvals, is
    A. Preliminary Phase
    B. Phase A: Architecture Vision
    C. Requirements Management
    D. All of the above
    E. None of the above

26. All of the following describe the Solutions Continuum except:
    A. The Solutions Continuum is a repository of re-usable solutions for future implementation efforts
    B. The Solutions Continuum is a part of the Enterprise Continuum
    C. The Solutions Continuum determines the content of the Architecture Landscape
    D. The Solutions Continuum The Solutions Continuum contains implementations of the corresponding definitions in the Architecture Continuum

27. Defining how the architecture constrains the implementation projects, monitoring it while building it, and producing a signed Architecture Contract is accomplished in
    A. Phase G
    B. Phase F
    C. Phase E
    D. Phase A

28. The objectives of Phase H include
    A. Ensuring that the architecture lifecycle is maintained
    B. Ensuring that the Architecture Governance Framework is executed
    C. Ensuring that the enterprise Architecture Capability meets current requirements
    D. All of the above

29. Architecture types (domains) typically include all of the following except:
    A. Business Architecture
    B. Strategy Architecture
    C. Application Architecture
    D. Data Architecture
    E. Technology Architecture

30. Regarding Transition Architectures, all of the following are true except:
    A. A Transition Architecture is a formal description of the enterprise architecture showing periods of transition and development for particular parts of the enterprise
    B. Ensures that the implementation project conforms to the architecture
    C. A Transition Architecture is used to provide an overview of current and target capability
    D. A Transition Architecture allows for individual work packages and projects to be grouped into managed portfolios and programs

31. Objectives of Phase G include
    A. Ensure conformance with the Target Architecture by implementation projects
    B. Ensure that the business value and cost of work packages and Transition Architectures is understood by key stakeholders
    C. Perform appropriate Architecture Governance functions for the solution and any implementation-driven architecture Change Requests
    D. A and C, above

32. The six parts of TOGAF include all of the following except:
    A. Part II: Architecture Development Method (ADM)
    B. Part IV: Architecture Content Framework
    C. Part V: Architecture Governance
    D. Part VI: Architecture Capability Framework

33. A time-bounded milestone for an organization used to demonstrate progress towards a goal (for example, "Increase Capacity Utilization by 30% by the end of 2009 to support the planned increase in market share") is
    A. A Goal
    B. A Vision
    C. An Objective
    D. A Transition Architecture Building Block

34. Categories of solution in the Solutions Continuum include all of the following except:
    A. Foundation
    B. Common Systems
    C. Business Sector
    D. Organization-Specific

35. A good business scenario is "SMART"
    A. Specific; Maintainable; Actionable; Realistic; and Time-bound
    B. Specific; Measurable; Achievable; Realistic; and Time-bound
    C. Specific; Measurable; Actionable; Robust; and Time-bound
    D. Specific; Measurable; Actionable; Realistic; and Time-bound

36. All of the following describe an Architecture Framework except:
    A. An Architecture Framework is a toolkit that can be used for developing a broad range of different architectures
    B. An Architecture Framework, ideally, describes a method for designing an information system in terms of a set of building blocks and for showing how the building blocks fit together
    C. An Architecture Framework, ideally, describes a method for aligning the organization's strategic plan, strategic objectives, and strategic performance indicators
    D. An Architecture Framework, ideally, contains a set of tools and provides a common vocabulary
    E. An Architecture Framework, ideally, includes a list of recommended standards and compliant products that can be used to implement the building blocks

37. An application component:
    A. Usually maintains a Data Component
    B. Is enabled by Technology Services
    C. Is Modular and Replaceable
    D. All of the above

38. Examples of Foundation Solutions include all of the following except:
    A. Programming languages
    B. Operating systems
    C. Enterprise management system products
    D. Generic approaches to organization structuring

39. Which of the following is not true about the Standards Information Base?
    A. Best practices create standards.
    B. External standards can be adopted by the enterprise.
    C. Standards have reference implementations.
    D. External reference models can be adopted by the enterprise.

40. All of the following describe Building Blocks except:
    A. A Building Block is a (potentially re-usable) component of business, IT, or architectural capability
    B. Building Blocks can be combined with other building blocks
    C. Building Blocks cannot be defined at various levels of detail, depending on what stage of architecture development has been reached
    D. Building blocks can relate to "architectures" or "solutions."

Test 4 Answers

1. The main aspects of the Preliminary Phase include all of the following except: **D. Developing a Target Business Architecture** Open Group Standard TOGAF® Version 9.2, 5.2, page 52
2. Applications use data and are supported by multiple technology components and are therefore part of the Technology Architecture. **B. False** Open Group Standard TOGAF® Version 9.2, 3.3, page 21
3. The description of a future state of the architecture being developed for an organization is referred to as the. **B. Target Architecture** Open Group Standard TOGAF® Version 9.2, 3.75, page 32
4. The objectives of Phase E, Opportunities and Solutions, include all of the following except: **C. Analyzing gaps** N181 Reference Card Page 13, Phase E under Objectives
5. Types of reference material provided by the Reference Library include all of the following except: **C. Selected products and services from suppliers** Open Group Standard TOGAF® Version 9.2, 37.3, page 393
6. Examples of artifacts include a network diagram, a server specification, a use-case specification, a list of architectural requirements, and a business interaction matrix. **A. True** Open Group Standard TOGAF® Version 9.2, 2.5, page 13
7. All of the following statements about Viewpoints are true except: **C. A View must be visual or graphical in nature** Open Group Standard TOGAF® Version 9.2, 3.18, page 23

8. Examples of Industry Solutions include

C. Both A and B, above

Open Group Standard TOGAF® Version 9.2, 35.4.2, page 382

---

9. Grouping projects into Transition Architectures is a key activity of

B. Phase E

N181 Reference Card Page 13 – Phase E under Objectives

---

10. Project establishment and initiating an iteration of the Architecture Development Cycle – setting the scope, constraints, and expectations for the iteration – is the purpose of the Preliminary Phase.

B. False

Open Group Standard TOGAF® Version 9.2, 5.1, page 52

---

11. Examples of Common Systems Architectures include all of the following except:

D. Foundation Architecture

Open Group Standard TOGAF® Version 9.2, 35.4.1, page 379

---

12. Types of reference material provided by the Reference Library include all of the following except:

D. Shared services already deployed within the organization

Open Group Standard TOGAF® Version 9.2, 37.3, page 393

---

13. The objectives of Phase B include all of the following except:

C. Validating business principles, goals, drivers, and Key Performance Indicators (KPIs)

Open Group Standard TOGAF® Version 9.2, 7.1, page 78

---

14. An organization is prepared to undertake successful enterprise architecture projects by the Preliminary Phase.

A. **True**

Open Group Standard TOGAF® Version 9.2, 5.2, page 52

---

15. An enterprise management system product and a security system product are examples of.

C. Common Systems Solutions

Open Group Standard TOGAF® Version 9.2, 35.4.2, page 381

16. Develop a high-level aspirational vision of the capabilities and business value to be delivered as a result of the proposed Enterprise Architecture is an objective of: **B. Phase A, Architecture Vision**   N181 Reference Card page 8, Phase A under Objectives
17. Required architectural changes that can normally be handled via change management techniques are referred to as   **A. Simplification change**   Open Group Standard TOGAF® Version 9.2, 15.5.2, page 162
18. Deliverables represent   **D. Both A and B, above**   Open Group Standard TOGAF® Version 9.2, 2.5, page 13
19. Defining the framework to be used is one of the main aspects of   **C. The Preliminary Phase**   Open Group Standard TOGAF® Version 9.2, 5.1, page 52
20. Once an Architecture Vision is defined and documented in the Statement of Architecture Work, it is critical to use the Architecture Vision to build a consensus, because   **B. Without this consensus it is very unlikely that the final architecture will be accepted by the organization as a whole**   Open Group Standard TOGAF® Version 9.2, 6.5.2, page 74
21. The objectives of Phase H include   **D. All of the above**   N181 Reference Card Page 16 – Phase H under Objectives
22. The major components within an Architecture Repository include all of the following except: **G. All of the above are components of an Architecture Repository**   Open Group Standard TOGAF® Version 9.2, 2.7, page 17

23. A useful way of assessing the ability of an enterprise to exercise different capabilities is through the use of
B. Capability Maturity Models (CMMs)
Open Group Standard TOGAF® Version 9.2, 5.5.7, page 62
24. Ensuring conformance with the Target Architecture by implementation projects is an objective of:
A. Phase G
N181 Reference Card Page 15 – Phase G under Steps and Objectives
25. The initial phase of an Architecture Development Cycle, which includes information about defining the scope, identifying the stakeholders, creating the Architecture Vision, and obtaining approvals, is
B. Phase A: Architecture Vision
Open Group Standard TOGAF® Version 9.2, 2.4, page 12
26. All of the following describe the Solutions Continuum except:
B. The Solutions Continuum determines the content of the Architecture Landscape
Open Group Standard TOGAF® Version 9.2, 3.71, page 31
27. Defining how the architecture constrains the implementation projects, monitoring it while building it, and producing a signed Architecture Contract is accomplished in
A. Phase G
N181 Reference Card Page 15 – Phase G under Objectives
28. The objectives of Phase H include
D. All of the above
Open Group Standard TOGAF® Version 9.2, 15.1, page 156
29. Architecture types (domains) typically include all of the following except:
B. Strategy Architecture
Open Group Standard TOGAF® Version 9.2, 2.3, pages 11-12

30. Regarding Transition Architectures, all of the following are true except:

B. Ensures that the implementation project conforms to the architecture

Open Group Standard TOGAF® Version 9.2, 3.80, page 33

31. Objectives of Phase G include

D. A and C, above

Open Group Standard TOGAF® Version 9.2, 14.1, page 150

32. The six parts of TOGAF include all of the following except:

C. Part V: Architecture Governance

Open Group Standard TOGAF® Version 9.2, 1.1, pages 4-5

33. A time-bounded milestone for an organization used to demonstrate progress towards a goal (for example, "Increase Capacity Utilization by 30% by the end of 2009 to support the planned increase in market share") is

C. An Objective

Open Group Standard TOGAF® Version 9.2, 3.54, page 29

34. Categories of solution in the Solutions Continuum include all of the following except:

C. Business Sector

Open Group Standard TOGAF® Version 9.2, 35.4.2, page 381

35. A good business scenario is "SMART"

D. Specific; Measurable; Actionable; Realistic; and Time-bound

Open Group Series Guide – Business Scenarios, Section 1, pages 1-2

36. All of the following describe an Architecture Framework except:

C. An Architecture Framework, ideally, describes a method for aligning the organization's strategic plan, strategic objectives, and strategic performance indicators

Open Group Standard TOGAF® Version 9.2, 1.3, page 8

37. An application component: **D. All of the above** Open Group Standard TOGAF® Version 9.2, 3.31, page 24
38. Examples of Foundation Solutions include all of the following except: **C. Enterprise management system products** Open Group Standard TOGAF® Version 9.2, 35.4.2, page 381
39. Which of the following is not true about the Standards Information Base? **D. External reference models can be adopted by the enterprise.** Open Group Standard TOGAF® Version 9.2, 37.4 page 394
40. All of the following describe Building Blocks except: **C. Building Blocks cannot be defined at various levels of detail, depending on what stage of architecture development has been reached** Open Group Standard TOGAF® Version 9.2, 3.23, page 24

TOGAF Level 1 Volume 1 Test 5

Questions

1. The Architecture Continuum shows the relationships among
   A. Foundational frameworks (such as TOGAF)
   B. Common system architectures (such as the III-RM)
   C. Industry architectures
   D. Enterprise architectures
   E. All of the above

2. The main aspects of the Preliminary Phase include all of the following except:
   A. Defining the architecture principles that will inform any architecture work
   B. Developing a Target Business Architecture
   C. Defining the framework to be used
   D. Defining the relationships between management frameworks

3. The benefits of Architecture Governance include
   A. Increased transparency of accountability, and informed delegation of authority
   B. Controlled risk management
   C. Protection of the existing asset base through maximizing re-use of existing architectural components
   D. All of the above

4. Concerns may pertain to any aspect of the system's functioning, development, or operation, including considerations such as
   A. Performance
   B. Reliability
   C. Security
   D. Distribution
   E. Evolvability
   F. All of the above

5. Providing continual monitoring and a change management process to ensure that the architecture responds to the needs of the enterprise and maximizes the value of the architecture to the business, is the objective of
   A. Phase H, Architecture Change Management
   B. Phase G, Architecture Governance
   C. Phase F, Migration Planning
   D. Phase E, Opportunities and Solutions

6. Specific areas to consider in the organizational context, identified in the Preliminary Phase, include all of the following except:
   A. The intentions and culture of the organization
   B. Architecture principles
   C. The stakeholders
   D. The commercial models and budget for the enterprise architecture

7. A specification that has been formally reviewed and agreed upon, that thereafter serves as the basis for further development or change is referred to as:
   A. A Baseline
   B. A Baseline Architecture
   C. The As-Is Architecture
   D. A Foundation Architecture
   E. None of the above

8. Developing architectures in the Business, Application, Data, and Technology domains is an objective of
   A. Phase B,
   B. Phases B and C
   C. Phases B, C and D
   D. Phases A, B, and C

9. Defining the constraining architecture principles is an objective of
   A. The Preliminary Phase
   B. Phase G, Implementation Governance
   C. Phase A, Architecture Vision
   D. Requirements Management

10. Key activities of Phase F include
    A. Finalizing a detailed Implementation and Migration Plan
    B. Performing a cost/benefit analysis and a risk assessment for projects identified in Phase E
    C. Generating and gaining consensus on an outline Implementation and Migration Strategy
    D. A and B, above
    E. A and C, above

11. All of the following statements about Architecture Viewpoints are true except:
    A. A definition of the perspective from which a view is taken
    B. An Architecture Viewpoint provides methods for classifying architecture and solution artifacts
    C. An Architecture Viewpoint is a specification of the conventions for constructing and using a view
    D. An Architecture Viewpoint is the vantage point or perspective that determines what you see

12. The objective of Phase H, Architecture Change Management, is to provide
    A. Continual monitoring
    B. A change management process
    C. A business process reengineering methodology
    D. All of the above
    E. A and B, above

13. Establishment of a Standards Information Base provides an unambiguous basis for architectural governance because:
    A. The standards are easily accessible to projects and therefore the obligations of the project can be understood and planned for
    B. Standards are stated in a clear and unambiguous manner, so that compliance can be objectively assessed
    C. Both A and B, above
    D. Neither A and B, above

14. Key activities of Phase G include all of the following except:
    A. Providing architectural oversight for the implementation
    B. Monitoring implementation work for conformance
    C. Grouping projects into Transition Architectures
    D. Producing a Business Value Realization

15. Developing the Baseline and Target Architecture and analyzing gaps is an objective of all of the following except:
    A. Phase B, Business Architecture
    B. Phase C, Information Systems Architectures (Application & Data)
    C. Phase D, Technology Architecture
    D. Architecture Change Management

16. An architectural representation of assets in use, or planned, by the enterprise at particular points in time is referred to as the
    A. Technical Reference Model
    B. Architecture Landscape
    C. Architecture Metamodel
    D. Architecture Capability

17. Objectives of Phase E include
    A. Generate the initial complete version of the Architecture Roadmap, based upon the gap analysis and candidate Architecture Roadmap components from Phases B, C, and D
    B. Determine whether an incremental approach is required, and if so identify Transition Architectures that will deliver continuous business value
    C. Define the overall solution building blocks to finalize the Target Architecture based on the Architecture Building Blocks (ABBs)
    D. All of the above

18. In the TOGAF Template for Defining Principles
    A. The "Name" element should represent both the essence of the rule and be easy to remember
    B. The "Statement" element should succinctly and unambiguously communicate the fundamental rule
    C. The "Rationale" element should highlight the business benefits of adhering to the principle, using business terminology
    D. The "Implication" element should highlight the requirements, both for the business and IT, for carrying out the principle – in terms of resources, costs, and activities/tasks
    E. All of the above

19. Examples of Common Systems Solutions include
    A. An enterprise management system product
    B. A security system product
    C. Both A and B, above
    D. Neither A nor B, above

20. Capability Architectures are used to
    A. Provide an overview of current capability
    B. Provide an overview of target capability
    C. Provide an overview of capability increments
    D. Allow for individual work packages and projects to be grouped within managed portfolios and programs
    E. All of the above

21. As part of Phase D, the architecture team must consider what relevant Technology Architecture resources are available in the Architecture Repository, in particular:
    A. Technology models relevant to Common Systems Architectures; for example, the III-RM
    B. Generic technology models relevant to the organization's industry "vertical" sector; for example, in the telecommunications industry such models have been developed by the TeleManagement Forum (TMF)
    C. The TOGAF Technical Reference Model (TRM)
    D. Existing IT services
    E. All of the above

22. Enterprise Architecture is a discipline used to integrate an enterprise into a _____ infrastructure to gain efficiency and effectiveness through processes such as structured_____, transparent_____, and other optimizing tools.
    A. Cohesive, change management, communications
    B. Broad, information flow, processes
    C. Cohesive, processes, information flow
    D. Broad, change management, communications

23. The Foundation Architecture
    A. Guides development of Foundation Solutions
    B. Is supported by Foundation Solutions
    C. Both A and B, above
    D. Neither A nor B, above

24. Bridging between the enterprise strategy and goals on the one hand, and the strategy and goals implicit within the current architecture reality is accomplished during
    A. Phase A
    B. Phase B
    C. Phases B, C, and D

25. A set of principles that reflect a level of consensus across the enterprise, and embody the spirit of thinking of existing enterprise principles is referred to as
    A. An architecture framework
    B. Architecture principles
    C. An architecture landscape
    D. Business drivers

26. The major components within an Architecture Repository include all of the following except:
    A. The Architecture Content Framework
    B. The Architecture Metamodel
    C. The Architecture Capability
    D. The Architecture Landscape
    E. The Standards Information Base (SIB)
    F. The Reference Library
    G. The Governance Log

27. Project establishment and initiating an iteration of the Architecture Development Cycle – setting the scope, constraints, and expectations for the iteration – is the purpose of
    A. The Preliminary Phase
    B. Phase A
    C. Phase E
    D. Requirements Management

28. Key considerations for the Data Architecture include all of the following except:
    A. Data Management
    B. Data Migration
    C. Data Transformation
    D. Data Governance

29. Categories of required architectural changes include all of the following except:
    A. Transformational change
    B. Simplification change
    C. Incremental change
    D. Re-architecting change

30. TOGAF methods can be integrated with
    A. ITIL
    B. CMMI
    C. COBIT
    D. PMBOK
    E. All of the above

31. TOGAF 9 can be used for developing a broad range of different enterprise architectures.
    A. True
    B. False

32. Ensuring that changes to the architecture are managed in a cohesive and architected way is a key activity of
    A. Phase G
    B. Phase H
    C. Phase E
    D. Phase F

33. A (potentially re-usable) component of business, IT, or architectural capability that can be combined with other building blocks to deliver architectures and solutions is referred to as
    A. A building block
    B. A deliverable
    C. An artifact
    D. Any of the above
    E. None of the above

34. A Transition Architecture
    A. Is a formal description of the enterprise architecture showing periods of transition and development for particular parts of the enterprise
    B. Sets the scope, constraints, and expectations for a TOGAF project
    C. Is used to provide an overview of current and target capability
    D. All of the above
    E. A and C, above

35. A summary formal description of the enterprise, providing an organizing framework for operational and change activity, and an executive-level, long-term view for setting direction is the Strategic Architecture.
    A. True
    B. False

36. Operating the Governance Framework is an objective of
    A. Phase G
    B. Phase H
    C. Requirements Management
    D. Phase F

37. Definition of the enterprise's business processes, organizational structure, and human capital assets is included in
    A. The Preliminary Phase
    B. Phase A: Architecture Vision
    C. Phase B: Business Architecture
    D. Requirements Management
    E. All of the above
    F. None of the above

38. A specification of the conventions for constructing and using a view (often by means of an appropriate schema or template) is referred to as
    A. A Concern
    B. An Artifact
    C. An Architecture Viewpoint
    D. A Building Block

39. The architecture and solution artifacts that an organization includes in its Architecture Repository are determined by the Enterprise Architecture.
    A. True
    B. False

40. A good enterprise architecture can bring important business benefits, including all of the following except:
    A. A more efficient IT operation
    B. More effective organizational performance metrics, measures, and dashboards
    C. Better return on existing investment
    D. Reduced risk for future investment

Test 5 Answers

1. The Architecture Continuum shows the relationships among **E. All of the above** Open Group Standard TOGAF® Version 9.2, 35.3, pages 376-77
2. The main aspects of the Preliminary Phase include all of the following except: **B. Developing a Target Business Architecture** Open Group Standard TOGAF® Version 9.2, 5.2, page 52
3. The benefits of Architecture Governance include **D. All of the above** Open Group Standard TOGAF® Version 9.2, 2.9, page 19
4. Concerns may pertain to any aspect of the system's functioning, development, or operation, including considerations such as **F. All of the above** Open Group Standard TOGAF® Version 9.2, 3.34, page 26
5. Providing continual monitoring and a change management process to ensure that the architecture responds to the needs of the enterprise and maximizes the value of the architecture to the business, is the objective of **A. Phase H, Architecture Change Management** N181 Reference Card Page 16, Phase H under Objectives and Steps
6. Specific areas to consider in the organizational context, identified in the Preliminary Phase, include all of the following except: **B. Architecture principles** Open Group Standard TOGAF® Version 9.2, 5.5.2, page 58
7. A specification that has been formally reviewed and agreed upon, that thereafter serves as the basis for further development or change is referred to as: **A. Baseline** Open Group Standard TOGAF® Version 9.2, 3.21, page 24

8. Developing architectures in the Business, Application, Data, and Technology domains is an objective of

C. Phases B, C and D

N181 Reference Card Pages 9 - 12

9. Defining the constraining architecture principles is an objective of

A. The Preliminary Phase

Open Group Standard TOGAF® Version 9.2, 5.1, page 52

10. Key activities of Phase F include

D. A and B, above

N181 Reference Card Page 14 – Phase F under Steps and Objectives

11. All of the following statements about Architecture Viewpoints are true except:

B. An Architecture Viewpoint provides methods for classifying architecture and solution artifacts

Open Group Standard TOGAF® Version 9.2, 3.18, page 23

12. The objective of Phase H, Architecture Change Management, is to provide

E. A and B, above

N181 Reference Card Page 16, Phase H under Objectives and Steps

13. Establishment of a Standards Information Base provides an unambiguous basis for architectural governance because:

C. Both A and B, above

Open Group Standard TOGAF® Version 9.2, 37.4.1, page 394

14. Key activities of Phase G include all of the following except:

C. Grouping projects into Transition Architectures

N181 Reference Card Page 15 – Phase G under Objectives, Steps, Inputs, and Outputs

15. Developing the Baseline and Target Architecture and analyzing gaps is an objective of all of the following except: **D. Architecture Change Management** N181 Reference Card Pages 9 - 12
16. An architectural representation of assets in use, or planned, by the enterprise at particular points in time is referred to as the **B. Architecture Landscape** Open Group Standard TOGAF® Version 9.2, 37.2, page 392
17. Objectives of Phase E include **D. All of the above** Open Group Standard TOGAF® Version 9.2, 12.1, page 132
18. In the TOGAF Template for Defining Principles **E. All of the above** Open Group Standard TOGAF® Version 9.2, 20.3, page 198
19. Examples of Common Systems Solutions include **C. Both A and B, above** Open Group Standard TOGAF® Version 9.2, 35.4.2, page 381
20. Capability Architectures are used to **E. All of the above** Open Group Standard TOGAF® Version 9.2, 37.2, page 392
21. As part of Phase D, the architecture team must consider what relevant Technology Architecture resources are available in the Architecture Repository, in particular: **E. All of the above** N181 Reference Card page 12, Phase D under Inputs

22. Enterprise Architecture is a discipline used to integrate an enterprise into a _____ infrastructure to gain efficiency and effectiveness through processes such as structured _____, transparent _____, and other optimizing tools.

A. Cohesive, change management, communications

Open Group Standard TOGAF® Version 9.2, 1.3 pages 6-8

---

23. The Foundation Architecture

C. Both A and B, above

Open Group Standard TOGAF® Version 9.2, 35.4.1, page 379

---

24. Bridging between the enterprise strategy and goals on the one hand, and the strategy and goals implicit within the current architecture reality is accomplished during

A. Phase A

Open Group Standard TOGAF® Version 9.2, 5.5.2, page 58

---

25. A set of principles that reflect a level of consensus across the enterprise, and embody the spirit of thinking of existing enterprise principles is referred to as

B. Architecture principles

Open Group Standard TOGAF® Version 9.2, 20.1, page 197

---

26. The major components within an Architecture Repository include all of the following except:

A. The Architecture Content Framework

Open Group Standard TOGAF® Version 9.2, 2.7, page 17

---

27. Project establishment and initiating an iteration of the Architecture Development Cycle – setting the scope, constraints, and expectations for the iteration – is the purpose of

B. Phase A

Open Group Standard TOGAF® Version 9.2, 6.5.1, page 73

---

28. Key considerations for the Data Architecture include all of the following except:

C. Data Transformation

Open Group Standard TOGAF® Version 9.2, 9.5, page 106

29. Categories of required architectural changes include all of the following except:
A. Transformational change
Open Group Standard TOGAF® Version 9.2, 15.5.2, page 162
30. TOGAF methods can be integrated with
E. All of the above
Open Group Standard TOGAF® Version 9.2, 2.10, page 20
31. TOGAF 9 can be used for developing a broad range of different enterprise architectures.
A. True
Open Group Standard TOGAF® Version 9.2, 1.3, page 8
32. Ensuring that changes to the architecture are managed in a cohesive and architected way is a key activity of
B. Phase H
N181 Reference Card Page 16 – Phase H under Objectives
33. A (potentially re-usable) component of business, IT, or architectural capability that can be combined with other building blocks to deliver architectures and solutions is referred to as
A. A building block
Open Group Standard TOGAF® Version 9.2, 2.5, page 13
34. A Transition Architecture
D. A and C, above
Open Group Standard TOGAF® Version 9.2, 3.80, page 33
35. A summary formal description of the enterprise, providing an organizing framework for operational and change activity, and an executive-level, long-term view for setting direction is the Strategic Architecture.
A. True
Open Group Standard TOGAF® Version 9.2, 3.74, page 32

36. Operating the Governance Framework is an objective of

B. Phase H

N181 Reference Card Page 16 – Phase H under Objectives

---

37. Definition of the enterprise's business processes, organizational structure, and human capital assets is included in

C. Phase B: Business Architecture

Open Group Standard TOGAF® Version 9.2, 2.4, page 12

---

38. A specification of the conventions for constructing and using a view (often by means of an appropriate schema or template) is referred to as

C. An Architecture Viewpoint

Open Group Standard TOGAF® Version 9.2, 3.18, page 23

---

39. The architecture and solution artifacts that an organization includes in its Architecture Repository are determined by the Enterprise Architecture.

A. True

Open Group Standard TOGAF® Version 9.2, 35.2, pages 375 - 376

---

40. A good enterprise architecture can bring important business benefits, including all of the following except:

B. More effective organizational performance metrics, measures, and dashboards

Open Group Standard TOGAF® Version 9.2, 1.3, pages 6-7

TOGAF Level 1 Volume 1 Test 6

Questions

1. An individual, team, or organization (or classes thereof) with interests in, or concerns relative to, the outcome of the architecture is referred to as
   A. An Actor
   B. A Customer
   C. A Stakeholder
   D. A Key Player

2. Foundation Solutions are
   A. Highly generic concepts, tools, products, services, and solution components
   B. Fundamental providers of capabilities
   C. Both A and B, above
   D. Neither A nor B, above

3. Governing and managing an Architecture Contract covering the overall implementation and deployment process is an objective of Phase H.
   A. True
   B. False

4. A process for deriving an organization-specific enterprise architecture that addresses business requirements is described in:
   A. Part II: Architecture Development Method (ADM)
   B. Part III: ADM Guidelines and Techniques
   C. Part IV: Architecture Content Framework
   D. Part V: Enterprise Continuum and Tools
   E. Part VI: Architecture Capability Framework

5. A Reference Model is
   A. An abstract framework for understanding significant relationships among the entities of [an] environment
   B. Based on a small number of unifying concepts and may be used as a basis for education and explaining standards to a non-specialist
   C. Is not directly tied to any standards, technologies, or other concrete implementation details
   D. All of the above

6. Examples of Common Systems Solutions include
   A. An operating system
   B. A foundational data structure
   C. A security system product
   D. A generic approach to organization structuring

7. The advantages that result from a good enterprise architecture can bring important business benefits, including: a more efficient IT operation; better return on existing investment, reduced risk for future investment; faster, simpler, and cheaper procurement.
   A. True
   B. False

8. Capabilities
   A. Are typically expressed in general and high-level terms
   B. Typically require a combination of organization, people, processes, and technology to achieve
   C. Both A and B, above
   D. Neither A nor B, above

9. Examples of Common Systems Architectures include
   A. Security Architecture
   B. Management Architecture
   C. Network Architecture
   D. All of the above

10. Specific areas to consider in the organizational context, identified in the Preliminary Phase, include
    A. The skills and capabilities of the enterprise
    B. The Baseline Architecture landscape
    C. Current processes that support execution of change and operation of IT
    D. The intentions and culture of the organization
    E. The stakeholders
    F. The commercial models and budget for the enterprise architecture
    G. All of the above

11. An Architecture View does not have to be visual or graphical in nature.
    A. True
    B. False

12. A defined, repeatable approach to address a particular type of problem is referred to as
    A. An Enterprise Continuum
    B. A Methodology
    C. A Method
    D. A Metamodel

13. The Architecture Continuum shows the relationships among all of the following except:
    A. Industry architectures
    B. Common system architectures (such as the III-RM)
    C. Transition architectures
    D. Enterprise architectures

14. Objectives of Phase A include
    A. Defining, scoping, and prioritizing architecture tasks
    B. Identifying stakeholders, their concerns, and objectives
    C. Defining business requirements and constraints
    D. All of the above

15. A structuring of Architecture Building Blocks (ABBs) that are re-usable architecture assets is represented by the Architecture Content Framework.
    A. True
    B. False

16. Objectives of Phase G, Implementation Governance, include all of the following except:
    A. Provide architectural oversight for the implementation
    B. Identification of major implementation projects, and grouping them into Transition Architectures
    C. Prepare and issue Architecture Contracts
    D. Ensure that the implementation project conforms to the architecture

17. Defining the enterprise is one of the main aspects of
    A. Phase A, Architecture Vision
    B. Phase B, Business Architecture
    C. The Preliminary Phase
    D. Requirements Management

18. Key activities of Phase G include
    A. Providing architectural oversight for the implementation
    B. Defining architecture constraints on implementation projects
    C. Governing and managing an Architecture Contract
    D. All of the above

19. Mobilizing supporting operations that will underpin the future-working lifetime of the deployed solution is an objective of Phase G.
    A. True
    B. False

20. The Enterprise Continuum consists of all of the following except:
    A. The Information Continuum
    B. The Enterprise Continuum
    C. The Architecture Continuum
    D. The Solutions Continuum

21. Objectives of the Preliminary Phase include
    A. Defining the constraining architecture principles
    B. Selecting and implementing supporting tools and other infrastructure to support the architecture activity
    C. Setting up a governance and support framework to provide business process and Architecture Governance through the ADM cycle
    D. All of the above

22. Objectives of Phase G include
    A. Performing appropriate governance functions while the system is being implemented and deployed
    B. Deriving a series of Transition Architectures that deliver continuous business value
    C. Ensuring conformance with the defined architecture by implementation projects and other projects
    D. A and C, above

23. A process for deriving an organization-specific enterprise architecture that addresses business requirements is described in the TOGAF Architecture Development Method.
    A. True
    B. False

24. The Architecture Landscape is divided into all of the following except:
    A. Strategic Architectures
    B. Segment Architectures
    C. Foundation Architectures
    D. Capability Architectures

25. Confirming the Transition Architectures defined in Phase E with the relevant stakeholders is an objective of
    A. Phase A
    B. Phase F
    C. Phase G
    D. Phase H

26. Highlighting a shortfall between the Baseline Architecture and the Target Architecture is the basic function of
    A. Requirements Management
    B. Architecture Vision
    C. Architecture Change Management
    D. Gap Analysis

27. The objectives of the Preliminary Phase include: preparing the organization for successful TOGAF architecture projects; and undertaking the preparation and initiation activities required to meet the business directive for a new enterprise architecture, including the definition of an Organization-Specific Architecture framework and tools, and the definition of principles.
    A. True
    B. False

28. Confirming the commitment of the stakeholders is an objective of.
    A. The Preliminary Phase
    B. Phase A, Architecture Vision
    C. Phase B, Business Architecture
    D. All of the above

29. Objectives of Phase E include
    A. Reviewing the target business objectives and capabilities, consolidating the gaps from Phases B to D, and then organizing groups of building blocks to address these capabilities
    B. Deriving a series of Transition Architectures that deliver continuous business value
    C. Generating and gaining consensus on an outline Implementation and Migration Strategy
    D. All of the above

30. Which of the following are benefits of the view creation process?
    A. Less work for the architects
    B. Better comprehensibility for stakeholders
    C. Greater confidence in the validity of the views
    D. All of the above are benefits

31. A Foundation Architecture is an architecture of building blocks and corresponding standards that supports all the Common Systems Architectures and, therefore, the complete enterprise operating environment.
    A. True
    B. False

32. The Data Architecture objectives of Phase C include
    A. Develop the Target Data Architecture that enables the Business Architecture and the Architecture Vision, while addressing the Request for Architecture Work and stakeholder concerns False
    B. Identify candidate Architecture Roadmap components based upon gaps between the Baseline and Target Data Architectures
    C. Neither of the above
    D. Both of the above

33. The criteria that distinguish a good set of principles are
    A. Specific, Measurable, Actionable, Realistic, and Time-bound
    B. Understandability, Robustness, Completeness, Consistency, and Coherence
    C. Understandability, Robustness, Completeness, Consistency, and Stability
    D. Understandability, Robustness, Completeness, Consistency, and Flexibility

34. A record of governance activity across the enterprise is provided by.
    A. The Governance Content Framework
    B. The Governance Information Database
    C. The Governance Log
    D. The Governance Repository

35. Ensuring that changes to the architecture are managed in a cohesive and architected way is a key activity of Phase G.
    A. True
    B. False

36. Key activities of Phase E include
    A. Identifying dependencies
    B. Assessing priorities
    C. Deciding on approach
    D. All of the above

37. Principles are an initial output of
    A. The Preliminary Phase
    B. Phase A, Architecture Vision
    C. Phase B, Business Architecture
    D. Requirements Management

38. A Baseline is described by all of the following except:
    A. Is a specification that has been formally reviewed and agreed upon
    B. Serves as the basis for further development or change
    C. Can be changed only through formal change control procedures or a type of procedure such as configuration management
    D. The existing defined system architecture before entering a cycle of architecture review and redesign

39. The major component of TOGAF that provides a model for structuring a virtual repository and provides methods for classifying architecture and solution artifacts, showing how the different types of artifacts evolve, and how they can be leveraged and re-used is the TOGAF Reference Model.
    A. True
    B. False

40. Assessing the performance of the architecture and making recommendations for change is an objective of
    A. Phase G
    B. Phase H
    C. Phase F
    D. Phase E

Test 6 Answers

1. An individual, team, or organization (or classes thereof) with interests in, or concerns relative to, the outcome of the architecture is referred to as

   C. A Stakeholder

   Open Group Standard TOGAF® Version 9.2, 3.72, page 31

2. Foundation Solutions are

   C. Both A and B, above

   Open Group Standard TOGAF® Version 9.2, 35.4.2, page 381

3. Governing and managing an Architecture Contract covering the overall implementation and deployment process is an objective of Phase H.

   B. False

   N181 Reference Card Page 15 – Phase G under Objectives

4. A process for deriving an organization-specific enterprise architecture that addresses business requirements is described in:

   A. Part II: Architecture Development Method (ADM)

   Open Group Standard TOGAF® Version 9.2, 4.1, page 37

5. A Reference Model is

   D. All of the above

   Open Group Standard TOGAF® Version 9.2, 3.59, page 29

6. Examples of Common Systems Solutions include

   C. A security system product

   Open Group Standard TOGAF® Version 9.2, 35.4.2, page 381

7. The advantages that result from a good enterprise architecture can bring important business benefits, including: a more efficient IT operation; better return on existing investment, reduced risk for future investment; faster, simpler, and cheaper procurement.

A. True

Open Group Standard TOGAF® Version 9.2, 1.3, page 7

8. Capabilities

C. Both A and B, above

Open Group Standard TOGAF® Version 9.2, 3.30, page 25

9. Examples of Common Systems Architectures include

D. All of the above

Open Group Standard TOGAF® Version 9.2, 35.4.1, page 379

10. Specific areas to consider in the organizational context, identified in the Preliminary Phase, include

G. All of the above

Open Group Standard TOGAF® Version 9.2, 5.5.2, page 58

11. An Architecture View does not have to be visual or graphical in nature.

A. True

Open Group Standard TOGAF® Version 9.2, 3.17, page 23

12. A defined, repeatable approach to address a particular type of problem is referred to as

C. A Method

Open Group Standard TOGAF® Version 9.2, 3.51, page 28

13. The Architecture Continuum shows the relationships among all of the following except:

C. Transition architectures

Open Group Standard TOGAF® Version 9.2, 35.4.1, page 378

14. Objectives of Phase A include

D. All of the above

N181 Reference Card page 8, Phase A under Objectives

15. A structuring of Architecture Building Blocks (ABBs) that are re-usable architecture assets is represented by the Architecture Content Framework.

B. False

Open Group Standard TOGAF® Version 9.2, 35.3, page 376

---

16. Objectives of Phase G, Implementation Governance, include all of the following except:

B. Identification of major implementation projects, and grouping them into Transition Architectures

N181 Reference Card Page 15, Phase G under Objectives

---

17. Defining the enterprise is one of the main aspects of

C. The Preliminary Phase

Open Group Standard TOGAF® Version 9.2, 5.5, page 57

---

18. Key activities of Phase G include

D. All of the above

N181 Reference Card Page 15 – Phase G under Objectives, Steps, Inputs, and Outputs

---

19. Mobilizing supporting operations that will underpin the future working lifetime of the deployed solution is an objective of Phase G.

A. True

N181 Reference Card Page 15 – Phase G under Steps and Objectives

---

20. The Enterprise Continuum consists of all of the following except:

A. The Information Continuum

Open Group Standard TOGAF® Version 9.2, 35.3, page 376

---

21. Objectives of the Preliminary Phase include

D. All of the above

Open Group Standard TOGAF® Version 9.2, 5.1, page 52

22. Objectives of Phase G include **D. A and C, above** N181 Reference Card Page 15 – Phase G under Objectives
23. A process for deriving an organization-specific enterprise architecture that addresses business requirements is described in the TOGAF Architecture Development Method. **A. True** Open Group Standard TOGAF® Version 9.2, 4.1.2, page 38
24. The Architecture Landscape is divided into all of the following except: **C. Foundation Architectures** Open Group Standard TOGAF® Version 9.2, 37.2, page 392
25. Confirming the Transition Architectures defined in Phase E with the relevant stakeholders is an objective of **B. Phase F** N181 Reference Card Page 14 – Phase F under Objectives
26. Highlighting a shortfall between the Baseline Architecture and the Target Architecture is the basic function of **D. Gap Analysis** Open Group Standard TOGAF® Version 9.2, 23.1, page 235
27. The objectives of the Preliminary Phase include: preparing the organization for successful TOGAF architecture projects; and undertaking the preparation and initiation activities required to meet the business directive for a new enterprise architecture, including the definition of an Organization-Specific Architecture framework and tools, and the definition of principles. **A. True** N181 Reference Card Page 6, Premlinary Phase under Objectives
28. Confirming the commitment of the stakeholders is an objective of. **A. The Preliminary Phase** Open Group Standard TOGAF® Version 9.2, 5.1, page 66

29. Objectives of Phase E include

D. All of the above

N181 Reference Card Page 13 – Phase E under Objectives and Steps

---

30. Which of the following are benefits of the view creation process?

D. All of the above are benefits

Open Group Standard TOGAF® Version 9.2, 31.2.2 page 323

---

31. A Foundation Architecture is an architecture of building blocks and corresponding standards that supports all the Common Systems Architectures and, therefore, the complete enterprise operating environment.

A. True

Open Group Standard TOGAF® Version 9.2, 35.4.1, page 378

---

32. The Data Architecture objectives of Phase C include

D. Both of the above

Open Group Standard TOGAF® Version 9.2, 9.1, page 97

---

33. The criteria that distinguish a good set of principles are

C. Understandability, Robustness, Completeness, Consistency, and Stability

Open Group Standard TOGAF® Version 9.2, 20.4.1, pages 199-200

---

34. A record of governance activity across the enterprise is provided by.

C. The Governance Log

Open Group Standard TOGAF® Version 9.2, 2.7, page 17

---

35. Ensuring that changes to the architecture are managed in a cohesive and architected way is a key activity of Phase G.

B. False

N181 Reference Card Page 16 – Phase H under Objectives

36. Key activities of Phase E include

D. All of the above

N181 Reference Card Page 13 – Phase E under Objectives and Steps

37. Principles are an initial output of

A. The Preliminary Phase

Open Group Standard TOGAF® Version 9.2, 5.4, page 56

38. A Baseline is described by all of the following except:

D. The existing defined system architecture before entering a cycle of architecture review and redesign

Open Group Standard TOGAF® Version 9.2, 3.21, page 24

39. The major component of TOGAF that provides a model for structuring a virtual repository and provides methods for classifying architecture and solution artifacts, showing how the different types of artifacts evolve, and how they can be leveraged and re-used is the TOGAF Reference Model.

B. False

Open Group Standard TOGAF® Version 9.2, 35.1, page 375

40. Assessing the performance of the architecture and making recommendations for change is an objective of

B. Phase H

N181 Reference Card Page 16 – Phase H under Objectives

TOGAF Level 1 Volume 1 Test 7

Questions

1. The standards with which new architectures must comply, which may include industry standards, selected products and services from suppliers, or shared services already deployed within the organization, are captured by.
   A. The Architecture Content Framework
   B. The Standards Information Base (SIB)
   C. The Architecture Repository
   D. The Architecture Metamodel
   E. The Reference Library

2. All of the following statements about Architecture Viewpoints are true except:
   A. An Architecture Viewpoint is a definition of the perspective from which a view is taken
   B. An Architecture Viewpoint is a specification of the conventions for constructing and using a view
   C. An Architecture Viewpoint is the vantage point or perspective that determines what you see
   D. An Architecture Viewpoint provides guidelines, templates, patterns, and other forms of reference material that can be leveraged in order to accelerate the creation of new architectures for the enterprise

3. Identification of major implementation projects, and grouping them into Transition Architectures, is an objective of Phase A, Architecture Vision.
   A. True
   B. False

4. Objectives of Requirements Management include
   A. Assessing the performance of the architecture and making recommendations for change
   B. Ensuring that the Requirements Management process is sustained and operates for all relevant ADM phases
   C. Managing architecture requirements identified during any execution of the ADM cycle or a phase
   D. B and C, above

5. Building blocks can be defined at various levels of detail and can be categorized as
   A. Architecture Building Blocks (ABBs)
   B. Solution Building Blocks (SBBs)
   C. Neither A nor B, above
   D. Both A and B, above

6. Developing the Baseline and Target Architecture and analyzing gaps is an objective of all of the following except:
   A. Phase B, Business Architecture
   B. Phase C, Information Systems Architectures (Application & Data)
   C. Phase D, Technology Architecture
   D. Phase E, Opportunities and Solutions

7. A Common Systems Architecture that focuses on the requirements, building blocks, and standards relating to the vision of Boundaryless Information Flow is the TOGAF Architecture Repository.
   A. True
   B. False

8. Architecture domains supported by TOGAF include:
   A. Business Architecture
   B. Data Architecture
   C. Application Architecture
   D. Technology Architecture
   E. All of the above

9. Regarding Architecture Views, all of the following are true except:
   A. An Architecture View is what is seen from a viewpoint
   B. An Architecture View may be represented by a model to demonstrate to stakeholders their
   C. An Architecture View provides guidelines, templates, patterns, and other forms of reference material that can be leveraged in order to accelerate the creation of new architectures for the enterprise
   D. An Architecture View does not have to be visual or graphical in nature

10. All of the following statements about a Common Systems Solution are true except:
    A. It is an implementation of a Common Systems Architecture that is composed of a set of products and services, which may be certified or branded
    B. It represents the highest common denominator for one or more solutions in the industry segments that the Common Systems Solution supports
    C. It is a fundamental provider of capabilities
    D. It provides organizations with operating environments specific to operational and informational needs, such as high availability transaction processing and scalable data warehousing systems

11. Assessing the performance of the architecture and making recommendations for change is an objective of Phase H.
    A. True
    B. False

12. The formulation of detailed sequence of Transition Architectures with a supporting Implementation and Migration Plan is addressed in Phase F: Migration Planning.
    A. The Preliminary Phase
    B. Phase A: Architecture Vision
    C. Phase E: Opportunities and Solutions
    D. Phase F: Migration Planning
    E. Phase G: Implementation Governance
    F. Phase H: Architecture Change Management
    G. Requirements Management

13. Strategic Architecture
    A. Refers to a summary formal description of the enterprise
    B. Provides an organizing framework for operational and change activity
    C. Is an executive-level, long-term view for direction setting
    D. All of the above

14. An example of an Industry Solution is
    A. An operating system
    B. An industry-specific point-of-service device
    C. A security system product
    D. A generic approach to organization structuring

15. The component of TOGAF that is based on the TOGAF Foundation Architecture and is specifically aimed at helping the design of architectures that enable and support the vision of Boundaryless Information Flow is the TOGAF Technical Reference Model.
    A. True
    B. False

16. An architecture of generic services and functions that provides a foundation on which more specific architectures and architectural components can be built is referred to as
    A. An As-Is Architecture
    B. A Generic Architecture
    C. A Foundation Architecture
    D. A Baseline Architecture

17. All of the following statements about a Common Systems Solution are true except:
    A. It is an implementation of a Common Systems Architecture that is composed of a set of products and services, which may be certified or branded
    B. It represents the highest common denominator for one or more solutions in the industry segments that the Common Systems Solution supports
    C. It is a fundamental provider of capabilities
    D. It represents a collection of common requirements and capabilities, rather than those specific to a particular customer or industry

18. Architecture principles are normally based in part on
    A. Governance principles
    B. Business principles
    C. Both A and B, above
    D. Neither A nor B, above

19. The objective of Phase H, Architecture Change Management, is to provide continual monitoring and a change management process to ensure that the architecture responds to the needs of the enterprise and maximizes the value of the architecture to the business.
    A. True
    B. False

20. A quantitative statement of business need that must be met by a particular architecture or work package is referred to as
    A. A Deliverable
    B. A Requirement
    C. A Constraint
    D. A Concern

21. Examples of Common Systems Architectures include all of the following except:
    A. Transition Architecture
    B. Security Architecture
    C. Management Architecture
    D. Network Architecture

22. Identifying stakeholders, their concerns, and objectives is an objective of
    A. Phase E
    B. Phase B
    C. Phase A
    D. The Preliminary Phase

23. An enterprise management system product and a security system product are examples of Organization-Specific Solutions.
    A. True
    B. False

24. Most reasons to constrain (or restrict) the scope of the architectural activity to be undertaken relate to limits in all of the following except:
    A. The organizational authority of the team producing the architecture
    B. The objectives and stakeholder concerns to be addressed within the architecture
    C. The availability of people, finance, and other resources
    D. The availability of Commercial Off-The-Shelf applications to support the business architecture

25. Articulating business requirements, cultural aspirations, organization intents, strategic intent, and/or financial requirements is accomplished in order for the sponsor to
    A. Identify the key decision makers
    B. Identify the key stakeholders
    C. Generate a Request for Architecture Work
    D. All of the above

26. Objectives of Phase G include
    A. Ensure that the Implementation and Migration Plan is coordinated with the enterprise's approach to managing and implementing change in the enterprise's overall change portfolio
    B. Ensure conformance with the Target Architecture by implementation projects
    C. Perform appropriate Architecture Governance functions for the solution and any implementation-driven architecture Change Requests
    D. B and C, above

27. Operating the Governance Framework is an objective of Requirements Management.
    A. True
    B. False

28. Categories of architecture in the Architecture Continuum include all of the following except:
    A. Strategic
    B. Common Systems
    C. Industry
    D. Organization-Specific

29. Identifying key drivers and elements in the organizational context is one of the main aspects of
    A. Phase A, Architecture Vision
    B. Phase B, Business Architecture
    C. The Preliminary Phase
    D. Requirements Management

30. Ensuring compliance with the defined architecture(s), not only by the implementation projects, but also by other ongoing projects, is a key aspect of
    A. Phase G
    B. Phase H
    C. Phase F
    D. Phase E

31. All of the following describe an Architecture Framework except:
    A. An Architecture Framework is a toolkit that can be used for developing one specific architecture
    B. An Architecture Framework, ideally, describes a method for designing an information system in terms of a set of building blocks and for showing how the building blocks fit together
    C. An Architecture Framework, ideally, contains a set of tools and provides a common vocabulary
    D. An Architecture Framework, ideally, includes a list of recommended standards and compliant products that can be used to implement the building blocks

32. The main aspects of the Preliminary Phase include
    A. Understanding the business environment
    B. Ensuring high-level management commitment
    C. Obtaining agreement on scope
    D. All of the above

33. Producing a Business Value Realization is a key activity of
    A. Phase A
    B. Phase G
    C. Phase B
    D. Phase E

34. Which of the following statements is not true?
    A. The Architecture Repository allows an enterprise to distinguish between different types of architectural assets
    B. The Architecture Repository is contained in the Enterprise Repository.
    C. There are six classes of architectural information in the Architecture Repository.
    D. The Enterprise Repository and the Architecture Repository are exclusive, but dependent upon each other.

35. A number of phases within a process of change illustrated by an ADM cycle graphic is called the
    A. Architecture Development Method (ADM)
    B. ADM Guidelines and Techniques
    C. Architecture Content Framework
    D. Enterprise Continuum and Tools
    E. TOGAF Reference Model
    F. Architecture Capability Framework

36. Objectives of the Preliminary Phase include all of the following except:
    A. Selecting and implementing supporting tools and other infrastructure to support the architecture activity
    B. Articulating an Architecture Vision and value proposition to respond to the requirements and constraints
    C. Defining an organization's "architecture footprint" – that is, the people responsible for performing the architecture work, where they are located, and their responsibilities
    D. Identifying stakeholders, their requirements, and their priorities

37. Creating, evolving, and monitoring the detailed Implementation and Migration Plan, providing necessary resources to enable the realization of the Transition Architectures, as defined in Phase E, is an objective of
   A. Phase A
   B. Phase F
   C. Phase G
   D. Phase H

38. The six parts of TOGAF include all of the following except:
   A. Part I: Introduction
   B. Part V: Enterprise Continuum and Tools
   C. Part VI: Architecture Capability Framework
   D. Part VI: Architecture Governance

39. Concerns may pertain to all of the following except:
   A. Any aspect of a system's functioning
   B. Any aspect of a system's cost
   C. Any aspect of a system's development
   D. Any aspect of a system's operation

40. Deciding on approach (e.g., make versus buy versus re-use; outsource; COTS; Open Source) is a key activity of
   A. Phase E
   B. Phase A
   C. Phase D
   D. The Preliminary Phase

Test 7 Answers

1. The standards with which new architectures must comply, which may include industry standards, selected products and services from suppliers, or shared services already deployed within the organization, are captured by **B. The Standards Information Base (SIB)** Open Group Standard TOGAF® Version 9.2, 2.7, page 17
2. All of the following statements about Architecture Viewpoints are true except: **D. An Architecture Viewpoint provides guidelines, templates, patterns, and other forms of reference material that can be leveraged in order to accelerate the creation of new architectures for the enterprise** Open Group Standard TOGAF® Version 9.2, 3.18, page 23
3. Identification of major implementation projects, and grouping them into Transition Architectures, is an objective of Phase A, Architecture Vision. **B. False** N181 Reference Card Page 8, Phase A under Objectives
4. Objectives of Requirements Management include **D. B and C, above** Open Group Standard TOGAF® Version 9.2, 16.1, page 166
5. Building blocks can be defined at various levels of detail and can be categorized as **D. Both A and B, above** Open Group Standard TOGAF® Version 9.2, 2.5, page 13
6. Developing the Baseline and Target Architecture and analyzing gaps is an objective of all of the following except: **D. Phase E, Opportunities and Solutions** N181 Reference Card Pages 9-12, under Steps

7. A Common Systems Architecture that focuses on the requirements, building blocks, and standards relating to the vision of Boundaryless Information Flow is the TOGAF Architecture Repository. **B. False** Open Group Standard TOGAF® Version 9.2, 35.4.1, page 378
8. Architecture domains supported by TOGAF include: **E. All of the above** Open Group Standard TOGAF® Version 9.2, 4.5.4, page 47
9. Regarding Architecture Views, all of the following are true except: **C. An Architecture View provides guidelines, templates, patterns, and other forms of reference material that can be leveraged in order to accelerate the creation of new architectures for the enterprise** Open Group Standard TOGAF® Version 9.2, 3.17, page 23
10. All of the following statements about a Common Systems Solution are true except: **C. It is a fundamental provider of capabilities** Open Group Standard TOGAF® Version 9.2, 35.4.2, page 381
11. Assessing the performance of the architecture and making recommendations for change is an objective of Phase H. **A. True** N181 Reference Card Page 16 – Phase H under Objectives
12. The formulation of detailed sequence of Transition Architectures with a supporting Implementation and Migration Plan is addressed in Phase F: Migration Planning. **D. Phase F: Migration Planning** N181 Reference Card Page 14 – Phase E under Objectives
13. Strategic Architecture **D. All of the above** Open Group Standard TOGAF® Version 9.2, 3.74, page 32

14. An example of an Industry Solution is

B. An industry-specific point-of-service device

Open Group Standard TOGAF® Version 9.2, 35.4.2, page 382

---

15. The component of TOGAF that is based on the TOGAF Foundation Architecture and is specifically aimed at helping the design of architectures that enable and support the vision of Boundaryless Information Flow is the TOGAF Technical Reference Model.

B. False

Open Group Standard TOGAF® Version 9.2, 35.4.1, page 379

---

16. An architecture of generic services and functions that provides a foundation on which more specific architectures and architectural components can be built is referred to as

C. A Foundation Architecture

Open Group Standard TOGAF® Version 9.2, 3.40, page 27

---

17. All of the following statements about a Common Systems Solution are true except:

C. It is a fundamental provider of capabilities

Open Group Standard TOGAF® Version 9.2, 35.4.2, page 381

---

18. Architecture principles are normally based in part on

B. Business principles

Open Group Standard TOGAF® Version 9.2, 5.5.4, page 59

---

19. The objective of Phase H, Architecture Change Management, is to provide continual monitoring and a change management process to ensure that the architecture responds to the needs of the enterprise and maximizes the value of the architecture to the business.

A. True

N181 Reference Card Page 16, Phase H under Objectives and Steps

---

20. A quantitative statement of business need that must be met by a particular architecture or work package is referred to as

B. A Requirement

Open Group Standard TOGAF® Version 9.2, 3.61, page 30

21. Examples of Common Systems Architectures include all of the following except:
A. Transition Architecture
Open Group Standard TOGAF® Version 9.2, 35.4.1, page 379

22. Identifying stakeholders, their concerns, and objectives is an objective of
C. Phase A
N181 Reference Card page 8, Phase A under Objectives

23. An enterprise management system product and a security system product are examples of Organization-Specific Solutions.
B. False
Open Group Standard TOGAF® Version 9.2, 35.4.2, page 382

24. Most reasons to constrain (or restrict) the scope of the architectural activity to be undertaken relate to limits in all of the following except:
D. The availability of Commercial Off-The-Shelf applications to support the business architecture
Open Group Standard TOGAF® Version 9.2, 4.5, page 44

25. Articulating business requirements, cultural aspirations, organization intents, strategic intent, and/or financial requirements is accomplished in order for the sponsor to
D. All of the above
Open Group Standard TOGAF® Version 9.2, 5.5.3, page 59

26. Objectives of Phase G include
D. B and C, above
Open Group Standard TOGAF® Version 9.2, 14.1, page 150

27. Operating the Governance Framework is an objective of Requirements Management.
B. False
N181 Reference Card Page 7 – Requirements Management under Objectives

28. Categories of architecture in the Architecture Continuum include all of the following except:

A. Strategic

Open Group Standard TOGAF® Version 9.2, 35.4.1, page 378

29. Identifying key drivers and elements in the organizational context is one of the main aspects of

C. The Preliminary Phase

Open Group Standard TOGAF® Version 9.2, 5.5.2, page 58

30. Ensuring compliance with the defined architecture(s), not only by the implementation projects, but also by other ongoing projects, is a key aspect of

A. Phase G

N181 Reference Card Page 15 – Phase G under Objectives

31. All of the following describe an Architecture Framework except:

A. An Architecture Framework is a toolkit that can be used for developing one specific architecture

Open Group Standard TOGAF® Version 9.2, 1.3, page 8

32. The main aspects of the Preliminary Phase include

D. All of the above

Open Group Standard TOGAF® Version 9.2, 5.2, page 57

33. Producing a Business Value Realization is a key activity of

B. Phase G

N181 Reference Card Page 15 – Phase G under Outputs

34. Which of the following statements is not true?

D. The Enterprise Repository and the Architecture Repository are exclusive, but dependent upon each other.

Open Group Standard TOGAF® Version 9.2, 37.1 page 391

35. A number of phases within a process of change illustrated by an ADM cycle graphic is called the **A. Architecture Development Method (ADM)** Open Group Standard TOGAF® Version 9.2, 1.1, page 4
36. Objectives of the Preliminary Phase include all of the following except: **B. Articulating an Architecture Vision and value proposition to respond to the requirements and constraints** Open Group Standard TOGAF® Version 9.2, 5.1, page 52
37. Creating, evolving, and monitoring the detailed Implementation and Migration Plan, providing necessary resources to enable the realization of the Transition Architectures, as defined in Phase E, is an objective of **B. Phase F** N181 Reference Card Page 14 – Phase F under Objectives
38. The six parts of TOGAF include all of the following except: **D. Part VII: Architecture Governance** Open Group Standard TOGAF® Version 9.2, 1.1, pages 4-5
39. Concerns may pertain to all of the following except: **B. Any aspect of a system's cost** Open Group Standard TOGAF® Version 9.2, 3.34, page 26
40. Deciding on approach (e.g., make versus buy versus re-use; outsource; COTS; Open Source) is a key activity of **A. Phase E** Open Group Standard TOGAF® Version 9.2, 24.2, page 240

TOGAF Level 1 Volume 1 Test 8

Questions

1. According to TOGAF, the order of the four phases of architecture development is:
   A. Foundation, Organization-Specific, Industry, Common Systems
   B. Foundation, Common Systems, Industry, Organization-Specific
   C. Foundation, Industry, Common Systems, Organization-Specific
   D. The order of the phases is not important.

2. In TOGAF, qualitative statements of intent that should be met by the architecture are referred to as
   A. The Architecture Vision
   B. Viewpoints
   C. Architecture Building Blocks
   D. Architecture Principles

3. Characteristics of an Architecture Model include all of the following except:
   A. An Architecture Model is a representation of a subject of interest
   B. An Architecture Model cannot be a representation of an entire enterprise
   C. An Architecture Model provides a smaller scale, simplified, and/or abstract representation of the subject matter
   D. An Architecture Model is constructed as a "means to an end"

4. Objectives of Phase E include all of the following except:
   A. Reviewing the target business objectives and capabilities, consolidating the gaps from Phases B to D, and then organizing groups of building blocks to address these capabilities
   B. Confirming the enterprise's capability for undergoing change
   C. Identifying and scoping the elements of the enterprise organizations affected and defining the constraints and assumptions
   D. Deriving a series of Transition Architectures that deliver continuous business value

5. A business scenario describes
   A. Real Business Problems and the business and technology environment in which those problems occur
   B. Value chains enabled by capabilities
   C. The human and computing components (the "actors") who provide the capabilities
   D. The desired outcome of proper execution
   E. All of the above

6. A (potentially re-usable) component of business, IT, or architectural capability that can be combined with other building blocks to deliver architectures and solutions is referred to as.
   A. A View
   B. An Artifact
   C. A Building Block
   D. A Baseline

7. Providing architectural oversight for the implementation, preparing and issuing Architecture Contracts, and ensuring that the implementation project conforms to the architecture are objectives of
   A. The Preliminary Phase
   B. Requirements Management
   C. Phase G, Implementation Governance
   D. Phase H, Architecture Change Management

8. Required architectural changes that may be capable of being handled via change management techniques, or that may require partial re-architecting, depending on the nature of the change, are referred to as
   A. Simplification change
   B. Incremental change
   C. Re-architecting change
   D. Transformational change

9. The architecture domains within TOGAF include:
   A. Business
   B. Data
   C. Application
   D. Technology
   E. All of the above

10. Objectives of Phase A, Architecture Vision, include all of the following except:
    A. Prepare the organization for successful TOGAF architecture projects
    B. Set the scope, constraints, and expectations for a TOGAF project
    C. Create the Architecture Vision
    D. Define stakeholders

11. The Architecture Continuum
    A. Offers a consistent way to define and understand the generic rules, representations, and relationships in an architecture, including traceability and derivation relationships
    B. Represents a structuring of Architecture Building Blocks (ABBs) that are re-usable architecture assets
    C. Shows the relationships among foundational frameworks (such as TOGAF), common system architectures (such as the III-RM), industry architectures, and enterprise architectures
    D. All of the above

12. Depending on the organization, principles may be established as any or all of the following except:
    A. Enterprise principles
    B. IT principles
    C. Technology principles
    D. Architecture principles

13. The Architecture Metamodel; the Architecture Capability; the Architecture Landscape; the Standards Information Base (SIB); the Reference Library; and the Governance Log are the major components within
    A. An Architecture Repository
    B. The Architecture Content Framework
    C. The Enterprise Continuum
    D. The TOGAF Reference Model
    E. None of the above

14. The objectives of Phase E, Opportunities and Solutions, include all of the following except:
    A. Developing architectures in the Business, Application, Data, and Technology domains
    B. Identify of delivery vehicles for the building blocks identified in the previous phases
    C. Identify major implementation projects
    D. Group major implementation projects into Transition Architectures

15. More detailed operating models for areas within an enterprise are provided by
    A. Segment Architectures
    B. Capability Architectures
    C. Both A and B, above
    D. Neither A nor B, above

16. An architectural oversight of the implementation is provided in
    A. The Preliminary Phase
    B. Phase A: Architecture Vision
    C. Phase E: Opportunities and Solutions
    D. Phase F: Migration Planning
    E. Phase G: Implementation Governance
    F. Phase H: Architecture Change Management
    G. Requirements Management

17. Preparing the organization for successful TOGAF architecture projects; and undertaking the preparation and initiation activities required to meet the business directive for a new enterprise architecture, including the definition of an Organization-Specific Architecture framework and tools, and the definition of principles are objectives of
    A. The Preliminary Phase
    B. Phase A, Architecture Vision
    C. Requirements Management
    D. All of the above

18. Typical providers of Common Systems Solutions include all of the following except:
    A. Business process outsourcing vendors
    B. "Software as a service" vendors
    C. Computer systems vendors
    D. Vendors of enterprise-specific software applications

19. Defining the framework and detailed methodologies that are going to be used to develop the enterprise architecture in the organization is an objective of.
    A. Phase A, Architecture Vision
    B. Phase B, Business Architecture
    C. The Preliminary Phase
    D. Requirements Management

20. The Architecture Continuum and the Solutions Continuum are complementary parts of
    A. The Architecture Metamodel
    B. The Architecture Content Framework
    C. The Enterprise Continuum
    D. The TOGAF Reference Model

21. A formal description of the enterprise architecture showing periods of transition and development for particular parts of the enterprise is referred to as
    A. A Transition Architecture
    B. As an Enterprise Architecture
    C. A Baseline Architecture
    D. A Foundation Architecture

22. Standards captured by the Standards Information Base may include all of the following except:
    A. Industry standards
    B. Selected products and services from suppliers
    C. Shared services already deployed within the organization
    D. Operating Systems

23. Key considerations for the Data Architecture include
    A. Data Management
    B. Data Migration
    C. Data Governance
    D. All of the above

24. A detailed, formal description of areas within an enterprise, used at the program or portfolio level to organize and align change activity, is referred to as a.
    A. A Solution Architecture
    B. An Architecture Continuum
    C. A Segment Architecture
    D. An Architecture Landscape

25. Typical providers of Common Systems Solutions include all of the following except:
    A. Business process outsourcing vendors
    B. Healthcare IT vendors
    C. "Software as a service" vendors
    D. Computer systems vendors

26. Objectives of Phase A include all of the following except:
    A. Obtaining management commitment for this particular cycle of the ADM
    B. Defining business requirements and constraints
    C. Understand the impact on, and of, other parallel Architecture Development Cycles
    D. Developing a Target Business Architecture

27. Key activities of Phase E include all of the following except:
    A. Identifying dependencies
    B. Identifying the major implementation projects
    C. Defining, scoping, and prioritizing architecture tasks
    D. Performing initial implementation planning

28. A Transition Architecture
    A. Is a formal description of the enterprise architecture showing periods of transition and development for particular parts of the enterprise
    B. Is used to provide an overview of current and target capability
    C. Allows for individual work packages and projects to be grouped into managed portfolios and programs
    D. All of the above

29. Examples of Foundation Solutions include all of the following except:
    A. Programming languages
    B. Operating systems
    C. Foundational data structures
    D. Security system products

30. The Architecture Vision provides a first-cut, high-level description of the Baseline and Target Architectures, covering
    A. The Business domain
    B. The Data domain
    C. The Application domain
    D. The Technology domain
    E. All of the above

31. Maximizing the business value from the architecture and ongoing operations is an objective of.
    A. Phase G
    B. Phase F
    C. Phase H
    D. Phase B

32. Categories of architecture in the Architecture Continuum include all of the following except:
    A. Foundation
    B. General Systems
    C. Industry
    D. Organization-Specific

33. Objectives of Phase A include all of the following except:
    A. Articulating an Architecture Vision and value proposition to respond to the requirements and constraints
    B. Creating a comprehensive plan in line with the project management frameworks adopted by the enterprise
    C. Analyzing the gaps between the Baseline and Target Architectures
    D. Obtaining formal approval to proceed

34. Ensuring that the program of solution is deployed successfully, as a planned program of work, is an objective of
    A. Phase E
    B. Phase F
    C. Phase G
    D. Phase H

35. Ensuring that the Requirements Management process is sustained and operates for all relevant ADM phases is an objective of
    A. Requirements Management
    B. The Preliminary Phase
    C. Phase A
    D. Phase B

36. A Common Systems Architecture that focuses on the requirements, building blocks, and standards relating to the vision of Boundaryless Information Flow is.
    A. The TOGAF Technical Reference Model (TRM)
    B. The TOGAF Integrated Information Infrastructure Reference Model (III-RM)
    C. The TOGAF Architecture Landscape
    D. The TOGAF Architecture Repository

37. Specific areas to consider in the organizational context, identified in the Preliminary Phase, include all of the following except:
    A. The skills and capabilities of the enterprise
    B. The Baseline Architecture landscape
    C. The Strategic Architecture Landscape
    D. Current processes that support execution of change and operation of IT

38. Monitoring the business and capacity management is a key activity of
    A. Phase H
    B. Phase F
    C. Phase E
    D. Phase B

39. In TOGAF, the ability for an organization to effectively undertake the activities of an enterprise architecture practice is referred to as a(n)
    A. Architecture Development Method (ADM)
    B. Architecture Content Framework
    C. Enterprise Continuum
    D. Reference Model
    E. Enterprise Architecture capability (or architecture capability)
    F. None of the above

40. Objectives of the Preliminary Phase include all of the following except:
    A. Setting up a governance and support framework to provide business process and Architecture Governance through the ADM cycle
    B. Identifying and scoping the elements of the enterprise organizations affected and defining the constraints and assumptions
    C. Defining and organizing an Architecture Development Cycle
    D. Confirming the commitment of the stakeholders

Test 8 Answers

1. According to TOGAF, the order of the four phases of architecture development is: **B. Foundation, Common Systems, Industry, Organization-Specific** Open Group Standard TOGAF® Version 9.2, 35.4.1 page 378
2. In TOGAF, qualitative statements of intent that should be met by the architecture are referred to as **D. Architecture Principles** Open Group Standard TOGAF® Version 9.2, 3.16, page 23
3. Characteristics of an Architecture Model include all of the following except: **B. An Architecture Model cannot be a representation of an entire enterprise** Open Group Standard TOGAF® Version 9.2, 3.15, page 23
4. Objectives of Phase E include all of the following except: **C. Identifying and scoping the elements of the enterprise organizations affected and defining the constraints and assumptions** N181 Reference Card Page 13 – Phase E under Objectives and Steps
5. A business scenario describes **E. All of the above** Open Group Standard TOGAF® Version 9.2, 23.4.1, pages 237-238
6. A (potentially re-usable) component of business, IT, or architectural capability that can be combined with other building blocks to deliver architectures and solutions is referred to as. **C. A Building Block** Open Group Standard TOGAF® Version 9.2, 3.23, page 24
7. Providing architectural oversight for the implementation, preparing and issuing Architecture Contracts, and ensuring that the implementation project conforms to the architecture are objectives of **C. Phase G, Implementation Governance** N181 Reference Card Page 15, Phase G under Objectives

8. Required architectural changes that may be capable of being handled via change management techniques, or that may require partial re-architecting, depending on the nature of the change, are referred to as **B. Incremental change** Open Group Standard TOGAF® Version 9.2, 15.5.2, page 162
9. The architecture domains within TOGAF include: **E. All of the above** Open Group Standard TOGAF® Version 9.2, 3.11 page 22
10. Objectives of Phase A, Architecture Vision, include all of the following except: **A. Prepare the organization for successful TOGAF architecture projects** N181 Reference Card Page 8, Phase A under Objectives
11. The Architecture Continuum **D. All of the above** Open Group Standard TOGAF® Version 9.2, 35.3, pages 376-377
12. Depending on the organization, principles may be established as any or all of the following except: **C. Technology principles** Open Group Standard TOGAF® Version 9.2, 20.1, page 197
13. The Architecture Metamodel; the Architecture Capability; the Architecture Landscape; the Standards Information Base (SIB); the Reference Library; and the Governance Log are the major components within **A. An Architecture Repository** Open Group Standard TOGAF® Version 9.2, 2.7, page 17
14. The objectives of Phase E, Opportunities and Solutions, include all of the following except: **A. Developing architectures in the Business, Application, Data, and Technology domains** N181 Reference Card Page 13, Phase E under Objectives

15. More detailed operating models for areas within an enterprise are provided by

A. Segment Architectures

Open Group Standard TOGAF® Version 9.2, 37.2, page 392

---

16. An architectural oversight of the implementation is provided in

E. Phase G: Implementation Governance

Open Group Standard TOGAF® Version 9.2, 2.4, page 12

---

17. Preparing the organization for successful TOGAF architecture projects; and undertaking the preparation and initiation activities required to meet the business directive for a new enterprise architecture, including the definition of an Organization-Specific Architecture framework and tools, and the definition of principles are objectives of

A. The Preliminary Phase

N181 Reference Card Page6, Preliminary Phase under Objectives

---

18. Typical providers of Common Systems Solutions include all of the following except:

D. Vendors of enterprise-specific software applications

Open Group Standard TOGAF® Version 9.2, 35.4.2, page 381

---

19. Defining the framework and detailed methodologies that are going to be used to develop the enterprise architecture in the organization is an objective of.

C. The Preliminary Phase

Open Group Standard TOGAF® Version 9.2, 5.1, page 52

---

20. The Architecture Continuum and the Solutions Continuum are complementary parts of

C. The Enterprise Continuum

Open Group Standard TOGAF® Version 9.2, 2.6, page 15

---

21. A formal description of the enterprise architecture showing periods of transition and development for particular parts of the enterprise is referred to as

A. A Transition Architecture

Open Group Standard TOGAF® Version 9.2, 3.80, page 33

22. Standards captured by the Standards Information Base may include all of the following except: **D. Operating Systems** Open Group Standard TOGAF® Version 9.2, 37.2, page 394
23. Key considerations for the Data Architecture include **D. All of the above** Open Group Standard TOGAF® Version 9.2, 9.5.1, page 106
24. A detailed, formal description of areas within an enterprise, used at the program or portfolio level to organize and align change activity, is referred to as a **C. A Segment Architecture** Open Group Standard TOGAF® Version 9.2, 3.64, page 30
25. Typical providers of Common Systems Solutions include all of the following except: **B. Healthcare IT vendors** Open Group Standard TOGAF® Version 9.2, 35.4.2, page 381
26. Objectives of Phase A include all of the following except: **D. Developing a Target Business Architecture** N181 Reference Card Page 8, Phase A under Objectives
27. Key activities of Phase E include all of the following except: **C. Defining, scoping, and prioritizing architecture tasks** N181 Reference Card Page 13 – Phase E under Objectives and Steps
28. A Transition Architecture **D. All of the above** Open Group Standard TOGAF® Version 9.2, 3.74, page 32
29. Examples of Foundation Solutions include all of the following except: **D. Security system products** Open Group Standard TOGAF® Version 9.2, 35.4.2, page 381

30. The Architecture Vision provides a first-cut, high-level description of the Baseline and Target Architectures, covering **E. All of the above** Open Group Standard TOGAF® Version 9.2, 6.5.2, page 75
31. Maximizing the business value from the architecture and ongoing operations is an objective of **C. Phase H** N181 Reference Card Page 16 – Phase H under Objectives
32. Categories of architecture in the Architecture Continuum include all of the following except: **B. General Systems** Open Group Standard TOGAF® Version 9.2, 35.4.1, page 378
33. Objectives of Phase A include all of the following except: **C. Analyzing the gaps between the Baseline and Target Architectures** N181 Reference Card page 8, Phase A under Objectives
34. Ensuring that the program of solution is deployed successfully, as a planned program of work, is an objective of **C. Phase G** N181 Reference Card Page 15 – Phase G under Steps
35. Ensuring that the Requirements Management process is sustained and operates for all relevant ADM phases is an objective of **A. Requirements Management** Open Group Standard TOGAF® Version 9.2, 16.1, page 166
36. A Common Systems Architecture that focuses on the requirements, building blocks, and standards relating to the vision of Boundaryless Information Flow is **B. The TOGAF Integrated Information Infrastructure Reference Model (III-RM)** Open Group Standard TOGAF® Version 9.2, 35.4.1, page 379

37. Specific areas to consider in the organizational context, identified in the Preliminary Phase, include all of the following except:

C. The Strategic Architecture Landscape

Open Group Standard TOGAF® Version 9.2, 5.5.2, page 58

---

38. Monitoring the business and capacity management is a key activity of

A. Phase H

N181 Reference Card Page 16 – Phase H under Steps

---

39. In TOGAF, the ability for an organization to effectively undertake the activities of an enterprise architecture practice is referred to as a(n)

E. Enterprise Architecture capability (or architecture capability)

Open Group Standard TOGAF® Version 9.2, 1.1, page 5

---

40. Objectives of the Preliminary Phase include all of the following except:

C. Defining and organizing an Architecture Development Cycle

Open Group Standard TOGAF® Version 9.2, 5.1, page 52

TOGAF Level 1 Volume 1 Test 9

Questions

1. Performing appropriate governance functions while the system is being implemented and deployed is an objective of
   A. Phase F
   B. Phase G
   C. Phase E
   D. Phase H

2. The six parts of TOGAF include all of the following except:
   A. Part I: Introduction
   B. Part II: Architecture Principles
   C. Part III: ADM Guidelines and Techniques
   D. Part IV: Architecture Content Framework

3. The process of managing architecture requirements throughout the ADM is examined in
   A. The Preliminary Phase
   B. Phase A: Architecture Vision
   C. Phase E: Opportunities and Solutions
   D. Phase F: Migration Planning
   E. Phase G: Implementation Governance
   F. Phase H: Architecture Change Management
   G. Requirements Management

4. Defining the relationships between management frameworks is one of the main aspects of
   A. Phase A, Architecture Vision
   B. Phase B, Business Architecture
   C. The Preliminary Phase
   D. Requirements Management

5. Providing architectural oversight for the implementation is a key activity of
   A. Phase E
   B. Phase F
   C. Phase G
   D. Phase H

6. Architecture types (domains) typically include:
   A. Business Architecture
   B. Application Architecture
   C. Data Architecture
   D. Technology Architecture
   E. All of the above

7. A model that describes how and with what the architecture will be described in a structured way is referred to as
   A. An Architecture Landscape
   B. A Metamodel
   C. An Architecture Continuum
   D. An Enterprise Continuum

8. In TOGAF, qualitative statements of intent that should be met by the architecture are referred to as Architecture Building Blocks.
   A. True
   B. False

9. The Architecture _____ highlights individual work packages' business value at each stage.
   A. Roadmap
   B. Transition Document
   C. Phase Development Document
   D. Milestones

10. Building blocks can relate to
    A. Architectures
    B. Solutions
    C. Frameworks
    D. All of the above
    E. A and B, above

11. A Solution Architecture is described by all of the following except:
    A. Typically applies to a single project or project release True
    B. Assists in the translation of requirements into a solution vision, high-level business, and/or IT system specifications
    C. Is a discrete and focused business operation or activity and how IS/IT supports that operation
    D. Typically applies to a portfolio of implementation tasks

12. The discipline of monitoring, managing, and steering a business (or IS/IT landscape) to deliver the business outcome required is referred to as Business Process Management.
    A. True
    B. False

13. Which of the following is not a benefit of well-established enterprise architecture?
    A. A more efficient business operation
    B. Better return on existing investment
    C. Reduced risk for future investment
    D. Faster, simpler, and cheaper process creation

14. "A collection of services, potentially an interface definition" is the definition of which term in the TOGAF 9.2 standard:
    A. Technology Service
    B. Value Stream
    C. Service Portfolio
    D. Business Capability

15. The Enterprise Continuum consists of
    A. The Enterprise Continuum
    B. The Architecture Continuum
    C. The Solutions Continuum
    D. All of the above

16. Identifying stakeholders, their concerns, and objectives is an objective of the Preliminary Phase.
    A. True
    B. False

17. A Building Block
    A. Is a (potentially re-usable) component of business, IT, or architectural capability
    B. Can be combined with other building blocks
    C. Can relate to "architectures" or "solutions."
    D. All of the above

18. The objectives of Phase E, Opportunities and Solutions, include all of the following except:
    A. Perform initial implementation planning
    B. Developing the Baseline and Target Architecture
    C. Identify major implementation projects
    D. Group major implementation projects into Transition Architectures

19. Categories of architecture in the Architecture Continuum include all of the following except:
    A. Foundation
    B. Common Systems
    C. Industry
    D. Enterprise-Specific

20. Assessing priorities is a key activity of Phase D.
    A. True
    B. False

21. TOGAF 9.2 defines a Stakeholder as:
    A. A person within the organization that has direct involvement with the system or process under review
    B. A member of the leadership team as defined in the Organization map
    C. An interested party who has an active involvement with a system
    D. An individual, team, organization, or class thereof, having an interest in a system.

22. Most reasons to constrain (or restrict) the scope of the architectural activity to be undertaken relate to limits in
    A. The organizational authority of the team producing the architecture
    B. The objectives and stakeholder concerns to be addressed within the architecture
    C. The availability of people, finance, and other resources
    D. All of the above

23. Reviewing the organizational context for conducting enterprise architecture is an objective of.
    A. The Preliminary Phase
    B. Requirements Management
    C. Phase A, Architecture Vision
    D. Phase B, Business Architecture

24. A Building Block represents a (potentially re-usable) component of business, IT, or architectural capability that can be combined with other building blocks to deliver architectures and solutions.
    A. True
    B. False

25. Developing architectures in the Business, Application, Data, and Technology domains is an objective of
    A. Phase B, Business Architecture
    B. Phase C, Information Systems Architectures (Application & Data)
    C. Phase D, Technology Architecture
    D. All of the above
    E. A and B, above

26. Types of reference material provided by the Reference Library include
    A. Guidelines
    B. Templates
    C. Patterns
    D. All of the above

27. The main aspects of the Preliminary Phase include
    A. Defining the enterprise
    B. Identifying key drivers and elements in the organizational context
    C. Defining the requirements for architecture work
    D. All of the above

28. A defined, repeatable approach to address a particular type of problem is referred to as a Metamodel.
    A. True
    B. False

29. The component of TOGAF that consists of a number of phases that cycle through a range of architecture domains that enable the architect to ensure that a complex set of requirements is adequately addressed is
    A. The Architecture Continuum
    B. The Architecture Framework
    C. The Architecture Development Method
    D. The Architecture Landscape

30. An organization is prepared to undertake successful enterprise architecture projects by.
    A. Requirements Management
    B. Phase A, Architecture Vision
    C. The Preliminary Phase
    D. Phase F, Opportunities and Solutions

31. Key activities of Phase E include
    A. Grouping projects into Transition Architectures
    B. Identifying the major implementation projects
    C. Performing initial implementation planning
    D. All of the above

32. Obtaining formal approval to proceed is an objective of Phase A.
    A. True
    B. False

33. At a high level, classes of architectural information that are expected to be held within an Architecture Repository include all of the following except:
    A. The Standards Information Base
    B. The Architecture Building Blocks and Solution Building Blocks
    C. The Reference Library
    D. The Governance Log

34. The Architecture Vision
    A. Provides the sponsor with a key tool to sell the benefits of the proposed capability to stakeholders and decision makers within the enterprise
    B. Analyzes the gaps between the Baseline and Target Architectures
    C. Provides a first-cut, high-level description of the Baseline and Target Architectures
    D. A and B, above
    E. A and C, above

35. Confirming the enterprise's capability for undergoing change is an objective of.
    A. The Preliminary Phase
    B. Phase A
    C. Phase E
    D. Phase H

36. Generating and gaining consensus on an outline Implementation and Migration Strategy is an objective of Phase E.
    A. True
    B. False

37. Computer systems vendors are the typical providers of
    A. Technology-centric Foundation Solutions
    B. Technology-centric Common Systems Solutions
    C. Technology-centric Industry Solutions
    D. Technology-centric Organization-Specific Solutions

38. The first phase that is directly concerned with implementation is
    A. Phases A, B, and C
    B. Phase D
    C. Phase E
    D. Phase F

39. Objectives of Requirements Management include
    A. Ensuring that relevant architecture requirements are available for use by each phase as the phase is executed
    B. Ensuring that the Requirements Management process is sustained and operates for all relevant ADM phases
    C. Ensuring that Baseline Architectures continue to be fit-for-purpose
    D. A and B, above

40. In TOGAF, Business Architecture refers to the business strategy, governance, organization, and key business processes information, as well as the interaction between these concepts.
    A. True
    B. False

Test 9 Answers

1. Performing appropriate governance functions while the system is being implemented and deployed is an objective of

B. Phase G

N181 Reference Card Page 15 – Phase G under Objectives

2. The six parts of TOGAF include all of the following except:

B. Part II: Architecture Principles

Open Group Standard TOGAF® Version 9.2, 1.1, pages 4-5

3. The process of managing architecture requirements throughout the ADM is examined in **G. Requirements Management** Open Group Standard TOGAF® Version 9.2, 2.4, page 12
4. Defining the relationships between management frameworks is one of the main aspects of **C. The Preliminary Phase** Open Group Standard TOGAF® Version 9.2, 5.2, page 52
5. Providing architectural oversight for the implementation is a key activity of **C. Phase G** N181 Reference Card Page 15 – Phase G under Objectives
6. Architecture types (domains) typically include: **E. All of the above** Open Group Standard TOGAF® Version 9.2, 2.3, pages 11-12
7. A model that describes how and with what the architecture will be described in a structured way is referred to as **B. A Metamodel** Open Group Standard TOGAF® Version 9.2, 3.50, page 28
8. In TOGAF, qualitative statements of intent that should be met by the architecture are referred to as Architecture Building Blocks. **B. False** Open Group Standard TOGAF® Version 9.2, 3.23, page 24
9. The Architecture _____ highlights individual work packages' business value at each stage. **A. Roadmap** Open Group Standard TOGAF® Version 9.2, 32.2.7 page 355
10. Building blocks can relate to **E. A and B, above** Open Group Standard TOGAF® Version 9.2, 3.23, page 24

11. A Solution Architecture is described by all of the following except: **C. Is a discrete and focused business operation or activity and how IS/IT supports that operation**   Open Group Standard TOGAF® Version 9.2, 3.69, page 31
12. The discipline of monitoring, managing, and steering a business (or IS/IT landscape) to deliver the business outcome required is referred to as Business Process Management.   **B. False**   Open Group Standard TOGAF® Version 9.2, 3.43, page 27
13. Which of the following is not a benefit of well-established enterprise architecture?   **D. Faster, simpler, and cheaper process creation**   Open Group Standard TOGAF® Version 9.2, 1.3, page 7
14. "A collection of services, potentially an interface definition" is the definition of which term in the TOGAF 9.2 standard: **C. Service Portfolio**   Open Group Standard TOGAF® Version 9.2, 3.68, page 31
15. The Enterprise Continuum consists of   **D. All of the above**   Open Group Standard TOGAF® Version 9.2, 35.3, page 376
16. Identifying stakeholders, their concerns, and objectives is an objective of the Preliminary Phase.   **B. False**   N181 Reference Card page 6, Preliminary Phase under Objectives
17. A Building Block   **D. All of the above**   Open Group Standard TOGAF® Version 9.2, 3.23, page 24
18. The objectives of Phase E, Opportunities and Solutions, include all of the following except: **B. Developing the Baseline and Target Architecture**   N181 Reference Card Page 13, Phase E under Objectives

19. Categories of architecture in the Architecture Continuum include all of the following except:

D. Enterprise-Specific

Open Group Standard TOGAF® Version 9.2, 35.4.1, page 378

---

20. Assessing priorities is a key activity of Phase D.

B. False

N181 Reference Card Page 12 – Phase D under Objectives

---

21. TOGAF 9.2 defines a Stakeholder as:

D. An individual, team, organization, or class thereof, having an interest in a system.

Open Group Standard TOGAF® Version 9.2, 3.72, page 31

---

22. Most reasons to constrain (or restrict) the scope of the architectural activity to be undertaken relate to limits in

D. All of the above

Open Group Standard TOGAF® Version 9.2, 4.5, 44

---

23. Reviewing the organizational context for conducting enterprise architecture is an objective of.

A. The Preliminary Phase

Open Group Standard TOGAF® Version 9.2, 5.1, page 52

---

24. A Building Block represents a (potentially re-usable) component of business, IT, or architectural capability that can be combined with other building blocks to deliver architectures and solutions.

A. True

Open Group Standard TOGAF® Version 9.2, 3.23, page 24

---

25. Developing architectures in the Business, Application, Data, and Technology domains is an objective of

D. All of the above

N181 Reference Card Pages 9-12 under Steps

26. Types of reference material provided by the Reference Library include

D. All of the above

Open Group Standard TOGAF® Version 9.2, 37.3, page 393

27. The main aspects of the Preliminary Phase include

D. All of the above

Open Group Standard TOGAF® Version 9.2, 5.5, page 57

28. A defined, repeatable approach to address a particular type of problem is referred to as a Metamodel.

B. False

Open Group Standard TOGAF® Version 9.2, 3.51, page 28

29. The component of TOGAF that consists of a number of phases that cycle through a range of architecture domains that enable the architect to ensure that a complex set of requirements is adequately addressed is

C. The Architecture Development Method

Open Group Standard TOGAF® Version 9.2, 2.4, page 12

30. An organization is prepared to undertake successful enterprise architecture projects by.

C. The Preliminary Phase

Open Group Standard TOGAF® Version 9.2, 5.5, page 57

31. Key activities of Phase E include

D. All of the above

N181 Reference Card Page 13 – Phase E under Objectives and Steps

32. Obtaining formal approval to proceed is an objective of Phase A.

A. True

N181 Reference Card page 8, Phase A under Objectives

33. At a high level, classes of architectural information that are expected to be held within an Architecture Repository include all of the following except:

B. The Architecture Building Blocks and Solution Building Blocks

Open Group Standard TOGAF® Version 9.2, 37.1, page 391

34. The Architecture Vision

E. A and C, above

Open Group Standard TOGAF® Version 9.2, 6.5.2, page 74

35. Confirming the enterprise's capability for undergoing change is an objective of.

C. Phase E

N181 Reference Card Page 13 – Phase E under Objectives

36. Generating and gaining consensus on an outline Implementation and Migration Strategy is an objective of Phase E.

A. True

N181 Reference Card Page 13 – Phase E under Objectives

37. Computer systems vendors are the typical providers of

B. Technology-centric Common Systems Solutions

Open Group Standard TOGAF® Version 9.2, 35.4.2, page 381

38. The first phase that is directly concerned with implementation is

C. Phase E

N181 Reference Card: ADM page 13, under Objectives

39. Objectives of Requirements Management include

D. A and B, above

Open Group Standard TOGAF® Version 9.2, 16.1, page 166

40. In TOGAF, Business Architecture refers to the business strategy, governance, organization, and key business processes information, as well as the interaction between these concepts.

A. True

Open Group Standard TOGAF® Version 9.2, 3.24, page 24

TOGAF Level 1 Volume 1 Test 10

Questions

1. Understanding the impact on, and of, other parallel Architecture Development Cycles is an objective of Phase A.
   A. All Phases of the TOGAF ADM
   B. Requirements Management
   C. Phase A
   D. The Preliminary Phase

2. The objectives of Phase H include
   A. Ensuring that Baseline Architectures continue to be fit-for-purpose
   B. Assessing the performance of the architecture and making recommendations for change
   C. Assessing changes to the framework and principles set up in previous phases
   D. Establishing an architecture change management process for the new enterprise architecture baseline that is achieved with completion of Phase G
   E. Maximizing the business value from the architecture and ongoing operations
   F. Operating the Governance Framework
   G. All of the above

3. Which of the following statement(s) is/are true?
   A. Architecture principles define the underlying general rules and guidelines for the use and deployment of all IT resources and assets across the enterprise.
   B. Architecture principles reflect a level of consensus among the various elements of the enterprise and form the basis for making future IT decisions.
   C. Each architecture principle should be clearly related back to the business objectives and key architecture drivers.
   D. All of the above
   E. None of the above

4. A time-bounded milestone for an organization used to demonstrate progress towards a goal (for example, "Increase Capacity Utilization by 30% by the end of 2009 to support the planned increase in market share") is an Objective.
   A. True
   B. False

5. Objectives of Phase A include all of the following except:
   A. Selecting tools and techniques for viewpoints
   B. Develop a high-level aspirational vision of the capabilities and business value to be delivered as a result of the proposed enterprise architecture
   C. Obtain approval for a Statement of Architecture Work that defines a program of works to develop and deploy the architecture outlined in the Architecture Vision

6. Categories of required architectural changes include all of the following except:
   A. Simplification change
   B. Transactional change
   C. Incremental change
   D. Re-architecting change

7. Initial implementation planning and the identification of delivery vehicles for the architecture defined in the previous phases is conducted during
   A. The Preliminary Phase
   B. Phase A: Architecture Vision
   C. Phase E: Opportunities and Solutions
   D. Phase F: Migration Planning
   E. None of the above

8. The Architecture Vision provides a first-cut, high-level description of the Baseline and Target Architectures, covering the Business, Data, Application, and Technology domains.
   A. True
   B. False

9. Key activities of Phase H include
   A. Ensuring that changes to the architecture are managed in a cohesive and architected way
   B. Monitoring implementation work for conformance
   C. Providing flexibility to evolve rapidly in response to changes in the technology or business environment
   D. A and C, above

10. IT benefits of Enterprise Architecture include all of the following except:
    A. More effective hiring of IT resources
    B. Better traceability of IT costs
    C. Lower IT costs
    D. Faster design and development
    E. Less complexity
    F. Less IT risk

11. A view of the Architecture Repository that provides methods for classifying architecture and solution artifacts as they evolve from generic Foundation Architectures to Organization-Specific Architectures is referred to as
    A. The TOGAF Reference Model
    B. The Enterprise Continuum
    C. The Architecture Continuum
    D. The Architecture Content Framework
    E. The Architecture Metamodel

12. Finalizing the Architecture Vision and Architecture Definition Documents, in line with the agreed implementation approach, is an objective of Phase A.
A. True
B. False

13. Objectives of Phase G include
A. Ensuring that the program of solution is deployed successfully, as a planned program of work
B. Ensuring conformance of the deployed solution with the Target Architecture
C. Confirming the enterprise's capability for undergoing change
D. A and B, above

14. Phase C: Information Systems Architectures is divided into several parts:
A. Application Architecture
B. Data Architecture
C. Security Architecture
D. All of the above
E. A and B, above

15. In which of the following are the data most extensive?
A. A data dictionary
B. A database
C. A Repository
D. A Data Library

16. In TOGAF, the key interests that are crucially important to the stakeholders in a system, and that determine the acceptability of the system, are referred to as Architecture Views.
A. True
B. False

17. What is an Enterprise?
A. A collection of organizations that share a common set of goals
B. A collection of organizations that have interlocking management structures
C. A collection of organizations that do business with one another
D. A collection of organizations that may not do business with one another, but that affect one another through their operations, products, or services
E. A collection of organizations operating in the same environment

18. In TOGAF, the structure of an organization's logical and physical data assets and data management resources is referred to as the
A. Information Systems Architecture
B. Data Architecture
C. Application Architecture
D. Technology Architecture

19. A summary formal description of the enterprise, providing an organizing framework for operational and change activity, and an executive-level, long-term view for setting direction is the
    A. Enterprise Architecture
    B. Foundation Architecture
    C. Strategic Architecture
    D. Baseline Architecture

20. A Requirement is a quantitative statement of business need that must be met by a particular architecture or work package.
    A. True
    B. False

21. Successful implementations of Architecture Contracts are delivered through _____.
    A. Architecture Governance
    B. Architecture Change Management
    C. Implementation Management
    D. Requirements Management

22. All of the following statements about Reference Models are true except:
    A. A Reference Model is an abstract framework for understanding significant relationships among the entities of [an] environment
    B. A Reference Model is based on a small number of unifying concepts and may be used as a basis for education and explaining standards to a non-specialist
    C. A Reference Model is directly tied to specific standards, technologies, or other concrete implementation details
    D. A Reference Model seeks to provide common semantics that can be used unambiguously across and between different implementations

23. The four categories of architecture in the Architecture Continuum are
    A. Strategic, Common Systems, Industry, Organization-Specific
    B. Foundation, Common Systems, Industry, Organization-Specific
    C. Foundation, General Systems, Industry, Organization-Specific
    D. Foundation, Common Systems, Business Sector, Organization-Specific
    E. Foundation, Common Systems, Industry, Enterprise-Specific

24. A capability is an ability that can be possessed by:
    A. An organization
    B. A person
    C. A system
    D. Any of the above

25. Ensuring that the business processes and policies (and their operation) deliver the business outcomes and adhere to relevant business regulation is the purpose of
A. Business Process Management
B. Business Governance
C. Business Architecture
D. Business Foundation

26. Most reasons to constrain (or restrict) the scope of the architectural activity to be undertaken relate to limits in all of the following except:
A. The extent of alignment of mission, vision, and business architecture
B. The organizational authority of the team producing the architecture
C. The objectives and stakeholder concerns to be addressed within the architecture
D. The availability of people, finance, and other resources

27. Examples of Common Systems Architectures include all of the following except:
A. Security Architecture
B. Management Architecture
C. Enterprise Architecture
D. Network Architecture

28. Assessing the dependencies, costs, and benefits of the various migration projects are activities in Phase F.
A. True
B. False

29. A specification that has been formally reviewed and agreed upon, that thereafter serves as the basis for further development or change and that can be changed only through formal change control procedures or a type of procedure such as configuration management is referred to as
A. An Architecture Principle
B. A Foundation
C. A Baseline
D. None of the above

30. A consistent way to describe and understand the implementation of the assets defined in the Architecture Continuum is provided by the
A. Architecture Framework
B. Solutions Continuum
C. Architecture Landscape
D. Solutions Platform

31. Objectives of the Preliminary Phase include all of the following except:
    A. Creating a comprehensive plan in line with the project management frameworks adopted by the enterprise
    B. Defining the constraining architecture principles
    C. Defining the framework and detailed methodologies that are going to be used to develop the enterprise architecture in the organization
    D. Confirming the commitment of the stakeholders

32. In TOGAF, an architectural work product that is contractually specified and in turn formally reviewed, agreed, and signed off by the stakeholders is referred to as an Artifact.
    A. True
    B. False

33. Identification of major implementation projects, and grouping them into Transition Architectures, is an objective of
    A. Phase A, Architecture Vision
    B. Phase E, Opportunities & Solutions
    C. Phase F, Migration Planning
    D. Phase H, Architecture Change Management

34. Key activities of the Preliminary Phase include
    A. Understanding the business environment
    B. Ensuring high-level management commitment
    C. Obtaining agreement on scope
    D. Establishing principles
    E. Establishing governance structure
    F. Agreeing on the architecture method to be adopted
    G. All of the above

35. Defining the architecture principles that will inform any architecture work is one of the main aspects of
    A. Phase A, Architecture Vision
    B. Phase B, Business Architecture
    C. The Preliminary Phase
    D. Requirements Management

36. A Solution Building Block is a candidate physical solution for an Architecture Building Block (ABB) – e.g., a Commercial Off-The-Shelf (COTS) package – that is a component of the Acquirer view of the architecture.
    A. True
    B. False

37. Developing the Baseline and Target Architecture and analyzing gaps is an objective of all of the following except:
A. Phase B, Business Architecture
B. Phase C, Information Systems Architectures (Application & Data)
C. Phase D, Technology Architecture
D. Migration Planning

38. Objectives of the Preliminary Phase include
A. Defining the framework and detailed methodologies that are going to be used to develop the enterprise architecture in the organization
B. Defining an organization's "architecture footprint" – that is, the people responsible for performing the architecture work, where they are located, and their responsibilities
C. Identifying and scoping the elements of the enterprise organizations affected and defining the constraints and assumptions
D. All of the above

39. Objectives of Phase E include all of the following except:
A. Reviewing the target business objectives and capabilities, consolidating the gaps from Phases B to D, and then organizing groups of building blocks to address these capabilities
B. Understand the impact on, and of, other parallel Architecture Development Cycles
C. Deriving a series of Transition Architectures that deliver continuous business value
D. Generating and gaining consensus on an outline Implementation and Migration Strategy

40. Performing initial implementation planning is a key activity of Phase A.
A. True
B. False

Test 10 Answers

1. Understanding the impact on, and of, other parallel Architecture Development Cycles is an objective of Phase A.   **C. Phase A**   N181 Reference Card page 8, Phase A under Objectives
2. The objectives of Phase H include   **G. All of the above**   Open Group Standard TOGAF® Version 9.2, 15.1, page 156
3. Which of the following statement(s) is/are true?   **D. All of the above**   Open Group Standard TOGAF® Version 9.2, 20.3, page 198
4. A time-bounded milestone for an organization used to demonstrate progress towards a goal (for example, "Increase Capacity Utilization by 30% by the end of 2009 to support the planned increase in market share") is an Objective.   **A. True**   Open Group Standard TOGAF® Version 9.2, 3.54, page 29
5. Objectives of Phase A include all of the following except: **A. Selecting tools and techniques for viewpoints**   Open Group Standard TOGAF® Version 9.2, 6.1, page 66
6. Categories of required architectural changes include all of the following except: **B. Transactional change**   Open Group Standard TOGAF® Version 9.2, 15.5.2, page 162
7. Initial implementation planning and the identification of delivery vehicles for the architecture defined in the previous phases is conducted during   **C. Phase E: Opportunities and Solutions**   Open Group Standard TOGAF® Version 9.2, 2.4, page 12

8. The Architecture Vision provides a first-cut, high-level description of the Baseline and Target Architectures, covering the Business, Data, Application, and Technology domains. **A. True** Open Group Standard TOGAF® Version 9.2, 7.5.2, page 89
9. Key activities of Phase H include **D. A and C, above** N181 Reference Card Page 16 – Phase H under Objectives
10. IT benefits of Enterprise Architecture include all of the following except: **A. More effective hiring of IT resources** Open Group Standard TOGAF® Version 9.2, 1.3, Page 7
11. A view of the Architecture Repository that provides methods for classifying architecture and solution artifacts as they evolve from generic Foundation Architectures to Organization-Specific Architectures is referred to as **B. The Enterprise Continuum** Open Group Standard TOGAF® Version 9.2, 2.6, page 15
12. Finalizing the Architecture Vision and Architecture Definition Documents, in line with the agreed implementation approach, is an objective of Phase A. **B. False** N181 Reference Card Page 8 – Phase A under Objectives
13. Objectives of Phase G include **D. A and B, above** N181 Reference Card Page 15 – Phase G under Objectives
14. Phase C: Information Systems Architectures is divided into several parts: **E. A and B, above** Open Group Standard TOGAF® Version 9.2, 2.4, page 12

15. In which of the following are the data most extensive? **C. A Repository** Open Group Standard TOGAF® Version 9.2, 3.60, page 30
16. In TOGAF, the key interests that are crucially important to the stakeholders in a system, and that determine the acceptability of the system, are referred to as Architecture Views. **B. False** Open Group Standard TOGAF® Version 9.2, 3.17, page 23
17. What is an Enterprise? **A. A collection of organizations that share a common set of goals** Open Group Standard TOGAF® Version 9.2, 1.3, page 6
18. In TOGAF, the structure of an organization's logical and physical data assets and data management resources is referred to as the **B. Data Architecture** Open Group Standard TOGAF® Version 9.2, 3.36, page 26
19. A summary formal description of the enterprise, providing an organizing framework for operational and change activity, and an executive-level, long-term view for setting direction is the **C. Strategic Architecture** Open Group Standard TOGAF® Version 9.2, 3.74, page 32
20. A Requirement is a quantitative statement of business need that must be met by a particular architecture or work package. **A. True** Open Group Standard TOGAF® Version 9.2, 3.61, page 30
21. Successful implementations of Architecture Contracts are delivered through _____. **A. Architecture Governance** Open Group Standard TOGAF® Version 9.2, 32.2.2 page 351

22. All of the following statements about Reference Models are true except:
C. A Reference Model is directly tied to specific standards, technologies, or other concrete implementation details
Open Group Standard TOGAF® Version 9.2, 3.59, page 29
23. The four categories of architecture in the Architecture Continuum are
B. Foundation, Common Systems, Industry, Organization-Specific
Open Group Standard TOGAF® Version 9.2, 35.4.1, page 378
24. A capability is an ability that can be possessed by:
D. Any of the above
Open Group Standard TOGAF® Version 9.2, 3.20, page 25
25. Ensuring that the business processes and policies (and their operation) deliver the business outcomes and adhere to relevant business regulation is the purpose of
B. Business Governance
Open Group Standard TOGAF® Version 9.2, 3.27, page 25
26. Most reasons to constrain (or restrict) the scope of the architectural activity to be undertaken relate to limits in all of the following except:
A. The extent of alignment of mission, vision, and business architecture
Open Group Standard TOGAF® Version 9.2, 4.5, page 44
27. Examples of Common Systems Architectures include all of the following except:
C. Enterprise Architecture
Open Group Standard TOGAF® Version 9.2, 35.4.1, page 379
28. Assessing the dependencies, costs, and benefits of the various migration projects are activities in Phase F.
A. True
N181 Reference Card Page 14 – Phase F under Outputs

29. A specification that has been formally reviewed and agreed upon, that thereafter serves as the basis for further development or change and that can be changed only through formal change control procedures or a type of procedure such as configuration management is

C. A Baseline

Open Group Standard TOGAF® Version 9.2, 3.21, page 24

---

30. A consistent way to describe and understand the implementation of the assets defined in the Architecture Continuum is provided by the

B. Solutions Continuum

Open Group Standard TOGAF® Version 9.2, 35.3, page 377

---

31. Objectives of the Preliminary Phase include all of the following except:

A. Creating a comprehensive plan in line with the project management frameworks adopted by the enterprise

Open Group Standard TOGAF® Version 9.2, 5.1, page 52

---

32. In TOGAF, an architectural work product that is contractually specified and in turn formally reviewed, agreed, and signed off by the stakeholders is referred to as an Artifact.

B. False

Open Group Standard TOGAF® Version 9.2, 3.37, page 26

---

33. Identification of major implementation projects, and grouping them into Transition Architectures, is an objective of

B. Phase E, Opportunities & Solutions

N181 Reference Card page 13, Phase E under Objectives

---

34. Key activities of the Preliminary Phase include

G. All of the above

Open Group Standard TOGAF® Version 9.2, 5.5, page 57

---

35. Defining the architecture principles that will inform any architecture work is one of the main aspects of

C. The Preliminary Phase

Open Group Standard TOGAF® Version 9.2, 5.5, page 57

36. A Solution Building Block is a candidate physical solution for an Architecture Building Block (ABB) – e.g., a Commercial Off-The-Shelf (COTS) package – that is a component of the Acquirer view of the architecture. **A. True** Open Group Standard TOGAF® Version 9.2, 3.70, page 31
37. Developing the Baseline and Target Architecture and analyzing gaps is an objective of all of the following except: **D. Migration Planning** N181 Reference Card Pages 9-12 under Steps
38. Objectives of the Preliminary Phase include **D. All of the above** Open Group Standard TOGAF® Version 9.2, 5.1, page 52
39. Objectives of Phase E include all of the following except: **B. Understand the impact on, and of, other parallel Architecture Development Cycles** N181 Reference Card Page 13 – Phase E under Objectives and Steps
40. Performing initial implementation planning is a key activity of Phase A. **B. False** N181 Reference Card Page 13 – Phase E under Steps

About the Authors

Steve Else, Ph.D., CEO, EA Principals, Inc.

As one of the world's foremost innovators, practitioners/consultants, lecturers, educators and trainers serving the Enterprise Architecture (EA) industry, Dr. Steve Else has been a sought-after authority within the global business transformation community for nearly two decades.

As Founder and CEO of EA Principals, Inc. (EAP), Dr. Else is among the globe's top TOGAF (The Open Group Architecture Framework) trainers, having worked with thousands of professionals to help them learn and practice EA. He is also author of the book Organization Theory and Transformation of Large, Complex Organizations.

In addition to leading EAP, he established and leads the Enterprise and Solution Architecture International Institute (ESAII) (esaii.org) under the Center for Public-Private Enterprise (CPPE) (cppe.org), which he founded in 1998. ESAII expands his global professional outreach and allows other experts to mentor students on complex, innovative enterprise solution approaches, going well beyond the enterprise architecture aspects of value delivery.

Offering a wealth of practical and academic experience to his EA, Open FAIR, TOGAF 9, and ArchiMate 2 Certification Training, (certified in the latter three, with individual training of 4,000+ professionals), Dr. Else is also a Certified Enterprise and Solutions Architect (BCS Professional Certifications), a Project Management Professional (PMP) and an FEAC Certified Enterprise Architect (CEA).

His clients have included the United Nations; national governments in the U.S., U.A.E., Oman, and Portugal; and U.S. State governments in Pennsylvania, California, Colorado and Virginia; as well as such top tier corporations such as GE, HP, Oracle, IBM, American Express, Pfizer, Microsoft, Johnson & Johnson, BB&T, the Federal Reserve Bank of New York, Cap Gemini, Cisco, Harley-Davidson, MasterCard, Nokia, Siemens, Boeing, Fannie Mae, the Bill & Melinda Gates Foundation, and the Howard Hughes Medical Institute.

Dr. Else is committed to helping cross-pollinate best business and technology practices as well as innovation throughout the government and between government and private sector entities. As part of his work at CPPE, he founded and is Executive Editor for The Government Transformation Journal (cppe.org) and founded and served as first Executive Editor of The EA Zone Journal.

He has also served in key EA consulting/practitioner roles, including BAE Systems, CSC, Dynamics Research Corp. and Synectics for Management Decisions in the private sector; as well as the Departments of Defense, Homeland Security, Transportation, and Health & Human Services in the public sector.

Teaching Enterprise Architecture, Business Intelligence, Information Systems Engineering Management, and Systems Engineering at the graduate level, especially at the University of Denver, University College (where he has taught over 30 courses in EA) is a way that Dr. Else continues to contribute his expertise and insights. He has taught Systems Analysis and Design, Technology Forecasting and Assessments, Knowledge Management, and Project and Change Management of several years.

As a passionate participant in the EA, IT, and Systems Engineering professional communities, Dr. Else is Founder and Chair of the Washington, D.C., Chapter of the Association of Enterprise Architects, Executive Editor of the Enterprise Architecture Professional Journal (http://eapj.org), Associate Editor of the Journal of Enterprise Architecture, and Assistant Director of Knowledge for the Technical Operations Board of the International Council on Systems Engineering (INCOSE.org).

Dr. Else is a retired U.S. Air Force pilot. Highlights of his career include serving as an Assistant Air Attaché in Paris, where he won a special medal for his work in the first Iraq War; receiving a high medal from the French and Brazilian governments; serving as an Air Force Liaison Officer in Germany; and his final Air Force assignment at the Pentagon, where he was Program Architect for Air Force business transformation, working in the Office of the Chief of Staff. Dr. Else piloted numerous aircraft (having begun flying at the age of 16 and becoming an instructor pilot at 19). He also holds an Airline Transport Rating in the Lear Jet and Boeing 717. As a pilot, he was an integral part of the mission that attempted to free the U.S. hostages held in Iran in 1979.

Dr. Else is married and lives in Alexandria, Virginia.

Michael J. Novak, COO, EA Principals, Inc.

Michael J. Novak is Chief Operating Officer of EA Principals, Inc., a global training and consulting firm. He is a retired U.S. Naval Officer and retired Federal Employee. His military career included service aboard ships of the Pacific Fleet; management of Equal Opportunity and Race Relations programs, intercultural relations/overseas diplomacy programs, shipboard training programs, and defense logistics. His significant duties included three command tours, service as an interpreter (Japanese-English) for the Director of Naval Intelligence, and on the staff of the Deputy Chief of Naval Operations, Logistics, in the Pentagon. His extensive career in government included positions with the Internal Revenue Service Office of Procurement, the IRS Office of Research, Department of the Treasury Office of Strategic Planning and Evaluation, the IRS Office of the National Director of Quality, and the Defense Logistics Agency Executive Directorate of Quality Assurance. His significant duties have included drafting the Treasury Department Strategic Plan; serving on task groups chartered by Vice President Gore's National Partnership for Reinventing Government; and developing and implementing Defense Department procurement policy.

Mr. Novak is a specialist in Organizational Performance Assessment and Improvement, particularly within the context of the Baldrige Criteria for Performance Excellence. His experience with the Baldrige Criteria and methodology began in 1994 as an Examiner with the President's Quality Award. Subsequently, he has served as Examiner, Team leader, Scorebook Editor, Team Mentor, and Judge in numerous Baldrige-based programs, and was a four-time Examiner with the Baldrige National Quality Award Program. He has been an internal and external consultant to organizations implementing the Baldrige method or applying for Baldrige-based awards. Currently, he is Executive Director of the Maryland Performance Excellence Awards program, a state-level Baldrige-based organizational excellence recognition program.

Mr. Novak has authored or co-authored five books and published nearly 100 professional papers, articles, and reviews, and has delivered over 80 presentations to industry, government, and professional audiences. He has been guest lecturer at colleges and universities including the University of Denver and the Johns Hopkins University Graduate Division of Business and Management and serves as a Facilitator for the U.S. Naval Academy Capstone Seminar in Moral Leadership. He has been interviewed on Federal News Radio and has been featured in periodicals such as Talent Management, Federal Computer Week, and Government Leader.

His writings have appeared in FedTech magazine, PMBoulevard, GOVTek Newsletter, EA Zone Journal, and the Government Transformation Journal.

Mr. Novak is a Past President of the Washington, DC, Chapter of the Knowledge Management Professional Society, and Past Co-Chair of the Federal Knowledge Management Working Group. He has also been Co-Chair of the Government Enterprise Integrators Group research team on Enterprise Risk Management and Co-Chair of the Knowledge and Human Capital Retention Special Interest Group. He is a graduate of the U.S. Naval Academy, the University of Maryland, and the U.S. Naval War College. He is a Senior Member of the American Society for Quality, a Certified Manager of Quality and Organizational Excellence, a Certified Quality Engineer, and a Certified Enterprise Architect.

Made in the USA
Monee, IL
29 May 2024